WalkBoston

More from AMC Books

Visit the AMC Online Store at **www.outdoors.org**

Exploring series:

Exploring in and around Boston on Bike and Foot, 2nd edition

Exploring the Hidden Charles

Exploring Martha's Vineyard by Bike, Foot, and Kayak, 2nd edition

Nature Walks series:

Nature Walks in Eastern Massachusetts, 2nd edition

More Nature Walks in Eastern Massachusetts

Nature Walks in Central and Western Massachusetts, 2nd edition

Nature Walks along the Seacoast

Nature Walks in Connecticut

Quiet Water and *Sea Kayaking* paddling series:

Sea Kayaking Coastal Massachusetts

Sea Kayaking along the New England Coast

Quiet Water Massachusetts/Connecticut/
Rhode Island: Canoe and Kayak Guide, 2nd edition

AMC River Guide: Massachusetts/Connecticut/
Rhode Island, 2nd edition

Other AMC titles:

Water Trails of Western Massachusetts

Discover the Berkshires of Massachusetts: AMC Guide to the
Best Hiking, Biking, and Paddling

Massachusetts Trail Guide, 8th edition

WalkBoston

Walking Tours of Boston's Unique Neighborhoods

Edited by
Robert Sloane
of WalkBoston

APPALACHIAN MOUNTAIN CLUB BOOKS
BOSTON, MASSACHUSETTS

Front Cover Photograph: Hancock Tower © Heath Robbins
                           www.heathrobbins.com
Back Cover Photographs: Boston Common © Kindra Clineff
                           www.kindraclineff.com
                           Boston Skyline © Getty Images
                           Gates at Harvard University © Heath Robbins

Cover Design: Mac & Dent

Book Design: Kristin Camp

Interior images by WalkBoston photographers unless otherwise noted.

Map Design: Kenneth Dumas

© 2003 WalkBoston. All rights reserved.

Distributed by The Globe Pequot Press, Inc., Guilford, CT.

LIBRARY OF CONGRESS-IN-PUBLICATION DATA
WalkBoston : walking tours of Boston's unique neighborhoods / compiled
and edited by Robert Sloane.
p.   cm.
ISBN 1-929173-36-9 (alk. paper)
1. Boston (Mass.)—Tours.   2. Walking—Massachusetts—Boston—
Guidebooks. 3. Neighborhood—Massachusetts—Boston—Guidebooks.
I. Title: Walk Boston.
II. Sloane, Robert, 1935-
F73.18.W36 2003
917.44'610444—dc21
2003008492

The paper used in this publication meets the minimum requirements of
the American National Standard of Information Sciences—Permanence
of Paper for Printed Library materials, ANSI Z39.48-1984.

Printed on recycled paper using soy-content inks. ♺

Printed in the United States of America.

10 9 8 7 6 5 4 3 2   04   05   06   07

 **contents**

III. Exploring Neighborhoods Outside Boston

IV. Long Walks, Paths, and Parks

V. Long Walks on the Oceanfront

⚐ acknowledgments

WALKBOSTON owes many thanks to the volunteer authors of the chapters in this book for their research and writings. Ann Hershfang and Regina Healy played essential review roles with their invaluable and thorough editing suggestions. Ken Dumas worked diligently and produced the marvelous maps. Ken Krause, WalkBoston's office manager, helped with writing and coordinating WalkBoston's annual walks. AMC publisher Beth Krusi and her staff Blake Maher and Belinda Thresher brought the book to life. Thanks are due to John Casagrande, attorney for WalkBoston, for establishing the framework for AMC/WalkBoston cooperation.

Readers and providers of information include Arlington: Doreen Stevens and JoAnn Robinson of the Arlington Historical Society; Howard Winkler; Richard Dyffy; Arlington Historical Commission. Boston: Nancy Richard and Sylvia Weedman of the Bostonian Society; Margaret Bratschi; Ed Gordon of the Victorian Society of America; Sheila Grove of the Washington Gateway Main Street; Robert Hayden of the University of Massachusetts; Polly Harrell of Boston Affiliates; Alan Hodges, author of *Boston on Foot City Planning Guide;* Ken Kruckemeyer; Randi Lathrop; Ellen Lipsey of the Boston Landmarks Commission; John Neale of the South End Historical Society. Brookline: Roger Reed and Greer Hardwick of the Brookline Preservation Commission; Linda Pehlke, author of *Exploring the Paths of Brookline.* Cambridge: Cara Seiderman of the Cambridge Community Development Department; Charles Sullivan and Sally Purrington Held of the Cambridge Historical Commission; Amanda Yost of Mount Auburn

Cemetery. Charles River: Sean Fisher of the Metropolitan District Commission. Chelsea: Chelsea Historical Commission; Chelsea Public Library; Nadine Mironchuk; Lewis Spence. Dedham: Jim Hanson and Ronald F. Frazier of the Dedham Historical Society. Deer Island: Marianne Connolly, Tim Watkins, and Barbara Allen of the Massachusetts Water Resources Authority; Dan Levin of the Conservation Law Foundation; Karen-Jayne Dodge and Nancy Farrell of Regina Villa Associates; Kevin Kirwin of the MIT Media Lab. Hull: Jim Lampke and Richard Cleverly (who provided Anne Kinnear's notes on Hull history). Lynn-Swampscott: Diane Shephard of the Lynn Historical Society. Neponset River: Catherine Garnett and Jim Kovich of the MDC; Valerie Burns of Boston Natural Area Network; Margaret Eckhardt; Society for the Preservation of New England Antiquities. Newton: David Olson of the Newton Historical Society. Roslindale: Andrea d'Amato of the Boston Transportation Department. Waltham: Robert Pollack; Karen LeBlanc of the Charles River Museum of History.

Special thanks are due to Howard/Stein-Hudson Associates for office support, encouragement, and participation in the preparation of the manuscript.

🚶 how to use this book

THE WALKS DESCRIBED in this book range from long to short, leafy to salty, hilly to flat, commercial to residential, open to urbanized. Each walk offers a unique take on urban areas, based on distinctive features of the greater Boston area. Whether you would like a long walk, a historic or architectural walk, or a walk that includes little-known areas and neighborhood gems, you will find examples of each in this book. Some are long, some are short, some offer alternative routes, some are accessible by wheelchair. Most start and end at public transportation. For basic guidance in your choices, they are grouped by five themes:

1. Tracing city history and change
2. Exploring the neighborhoods of Boston
3. Exploring neighborhoods outside Boston
4. Long walks, paths, and parks
5. Long walks on the oceanfront

Inside the great ring road of Route 128/I-95 are more than thirty cities and towns, each with a unique character, with neighborhoods that are identifiable to local people and to you, once you have seen them. Boston prides itself on being a walker's city. It is quite simply a wonderful place to walk, densely built up with historic old buildings—a city of neighborhoods with those New England specialties of greens, church steeples, quaint houses, salt air, and Revolutionary War sites. The remarkable thing is that so many cities and towns near Boston share these traits. Here, in this book, you are offered many choices of places to walk—in Boston's walkable neighborhoods, of course, but also in equally interesting, smaller, and less well-known paths in other cities and towns.

The thirty walks in this book have been designed by WalkBoston members, and most have been led by and for WalkBoston members. The writers describe their own neighborhoods and places they know well and love. The walks are individual and special. For walks that are better known, such as the Freedom Trail, the last chapter of the book includes telephone numbers and addresses for sponsoring organizations.

Using the Walk Maps

Maps in this book show you exact routes for each walk, including major streets, cross streets, and shortcuts back to your starting place. There are variations in some walks, and the maps can help you plan shorter versions of the routes. Alternative—usually shorter—routes are shown. Diversions are also possible; walkers should be encouraged to look at an interesting building or street in more detail. After a diversion, use the maps to find your way back to the mapped route.

On each map the walk's starting and ending points are clearly indicated, with the route of the walk between. The map shows the location of essential facilities—public transportation stops and public rest rooms. Not shown are commercial locations, such as restaurants, as these are subject to change from year to year. In some instances the text mentions specific eating places or shops because of their historic importance to the neighborhoods they serve.

WalkBoston volunteers test-walked each of the walks to make sure that the estimated times and distances are generally correct. But of, course, people's paces and wanderings vary.

Walking on Public Ways

These walks have been designed with the walker's convenience in mind and are almost always along paved walkways.

(The nonpaved walks are usually on hard-packed public beaches.) In town and city centers you will usually find curb cuts for wheeled vehicles, such as wheelchairs or baby carriages. Signalized intersections customarily include **WALK** and **DON'T WALK** lights, and now include countdown lights that remind walkers of the time remaining to cross safely. In many locations buttons must be pushed to get a **WALK** light. At stop signs pedestrians should watch for oncoming traffic before crossing the street: Massachusetts drivers' behavior varies considerably.

Using Public Transportation

Public transportation is a walker's best friend, and these walks have been designed for it. Of course, you can get to the beginning of each of the walks in this book by driving, but it isn't as much fun. Public transportation extends the walking experience and sense of adventure associated with new places. And it is a relatively inexpensive way to travel.

In the Boston area you can get to nearly every community inside Route 128 via public transportation—bus, streetcar, subway, commuter train, or ferry. You need to know and understand the network of routes that will help you get to the start of your walk. This involves looking at the MBTA system map, finding where you want to go, and determining which line will take you there. The system map also indicates transportation routes provided by private companies to reach places such as Deer Island and Hull. MBTA maps, schedules, and fares are available by calling the MBTA at (617) 222-5000 or online at www.MBTA.com. MBTA service may be reduced on weekends—particularly on Sunday. Some services, such as ferries, may be operated seasonally and unavailable during colder months.

Even if you drive, you can use public transportation. Park near the public transportation station where the walk begins;

then, when you have finished the walk, use public transportation to get back to your starting point.

What to Take on a Walk

Assuming that you have appropriate shoes and clothing for walking, you should be reminded that a hat is a good thing to have on a hot day. Avoid dehydration by carrying along water on all your walks, even though public water sources may be listed for the walk of your choice.

Avoid stress by allotting enough time to get to and from the walking route and to complete the walk you choose. Take time out to rest if you tire; one method is to come to a full stop as you look at a point of interest. Or find a good place to sit—a bench, a doorstep, a bus stop—while you contemplate your day's rewards.

It makes sense to walk during daylight hours, if you can. Take along a companion and enjoy the walk.

What to Look For on a Walk

Members of WalkBoston believe that most—if not all—communities are walkable. After taking one of the walks in this book, we hope that you will agree that it is enjoyable to walk almost anywhere—not just in parks or open spaces but in urbanized communities. We also hope that you will become more aware of pedestrian needs: you may begin to note changes that should be made to protect children and older walkers. Traffic signals, sidewalk maintenance, and well-placed, marked crosswalks are important for walkers, and you may want to report their absence to a local governmental agency.

So select a walk to clear your head, aid digestion, provide pleasure and exertion, and explore new places on foot.

introduction

A Peripatetic (What Else?) Guide to Walking

WALKING DEFINES our humanity, amplifies our curiosity, and shapes our destiny. As an ambulatory species and intellectual hunter-gatherer of things ordinary and extraordinary, mental and menial, you might say that we are what we walk.

This is the precept that has persuaded WalkBoston, the nation's first pedestrian advocacy organization, and the Appalachian Mountain Club, the nation's oldest conservation and recreation organization, to launch you on a trip through what we chauvinistically believe is the nation's premier pedestrian world.

You, as a sturdy walker or novice pedestrian, are about to follow paths that will not only lead you through historic and contemporary places but *demand* that you do so in the most human way: one foot in front of the other. It is this act that allows us bipeds to get the footprint and feel of the past and present life of this great and extended city. By taking you on a walk through the history and scenery of thirty neighborhoods via this most everyday of motions, Boston's premier pedestrian organization emphasizes that a pedestrian—that is, human—approach is the historic source and enduring sense of greater Boston.

"A traveler on foot in this country seems to be considered as a sort of wildman, or an out-of-the-way being who is stared at, pitied, suspected and shunned by everybody that he meets," an eighteenth-century foot traveler once noted.

Today's harassed walkers will find that this is distinctly not so on these tours.

Demonstrating that walking is the wave of the future, WalkBoston's multifarious authors serve as guides to take you to eye-opening vistas, engaging sights, and mind-widening explorations. On foot. Our member-writers let you bear witness to not only the splendor but also the quirks of the workaday; you will also see quiet eras savored by walking within the circumferential highway of Route 128 that defines metropolitan Boston. Forget the windshield view. Our member-writers stretch the usual tourist map, relying on the public transportation that shaped this venerable city as it created the pre-automobile era.

The walks, all happily manageable without a car, show off the work of the city's builders. Boston remains a streetcar city, offering the diversity and mobility to broaden your personal range of motion. WalkBoston's approach is supported by a web of rail and public transportation taking you to far-flung corners on foot, not car, in this well-connected, human-scaled metropolis.

Using the Guide's Sites and Sights

Through this original guide, WalkBoston hopes readers and walkers will appreciate the diversity, history, and architectural neighborliness of these sites. These guided visits invite you to recall the troop movement of the Revolutionary War or consider the long timeline of the landscape at a screw factory at Newton Upper Falls on land purchased from Chief Nahatan.

There are no conventional "so-and-so slept here" routes, however. Our opening jaunt rejects a "Disney-fied" view of Boston to reveal a good or "ghastly deed lurking around every corner." (Even natives familiar with the venerable collection at the Boston Athenaeum may be aghast to find a human-skin-bound book amid its more scholarly and aesthetic treasures.) Moving from "then" to "now" to "then" in fascinating proximity, WalkBoston's journeys offer innumerable built and natural landscapes. You can tour the stately mansion of the Shirley-Eustis House in Roxbury or catch the whiff of the sea on the beach at Savin Hill and view countless sites compressing history on a narrow landmass with modern conveniences.

WalkBoston's veneration for this city is clear. How many other metropolises could proffer a *Baedeker* of urban life that sends you scuttling from the close-packed downtown . . . to the top of Brookline's Corey Hill . . . to the year-round summer-cottage-style delights of Hull on the periphery . . . to the mill sites of Newton and Milton? Where else can you pace off the residue of four centuries written in the landscape of rivers dammed, gravel transported to fill the bay, prominences left from the glacial residue, and the artistry of planners and architects in shaping stone or green space?

Trotting Out on Foot

Walking Bostonians (and WalkBoston) take pride in moments of *contemporary* activism embedded in both the old and new lines of pedestrian movement that carry the reader-walker through unique journeys. A walk down the splendid Southwest Corridor is a testament to the act of political will by which Boston's communities stopped a highway, diverting funds to plant this 5-mile park atop Back Bay's railroad. WalkBoston guides you along this route as it traverses city and suburbs, from the South End to Jamaica Plain to Forest Hills, with a return trip by the Orange Line subway.

Of varied length, other walkways—including the Minuteman Rail-Trail through Cambridge, Arlington, and Lexington, atop Brookline's and Boston's peaks, or along the Charles River—forge a place for our guided tourists to walk. The longest journey takes you to a western point of the Charles River where migrating shad, congregating gulls, and cormorants are abundantly on view with the Charles River Museum of Industry nearby.

Relief is at hand for the foot-weary, however. Each excursion also offers the opportunity to take a "Rosie Ruiz" escape route made famous, or infamous, by the legendary runner who ducked out of the prescribed route of the Boston Marathon, using the subway to leapfrog over the first-place runner and "win" the women's category in 1980. So, too, these outings enable you to walk and take the T for a power return.

Getting On with It

On your mark, then, book in hand: Get set. Go.

Don't expect this book to prescribe a formula for your walk. As distinctive as the various authors who decided what places and what paces the reader will tread, so, too, do the style and content vary in this idiosyncratic and personal book. The timing is theirs, but the choice is yours. Your own pace—defined by fatigue, fascination, and the four seasons—will determine your distance.

Go through the paces of these walks and you'll find transportation to carry you back home after an outing certain to leave you informed, restored, and reinvigorated by this more mobile, and, yes, more humanized view of Boston's "City Upon a Hill." Bon voyage and enjoy the pedestrian view.

JANE HOLTZ KAY *is author of* Asphalt Nation: How the Automobile Took Over America and How We Can Take It Back *and* Lost Boston.

part 1

Tracing City History and Change

 **walk 1**

Disasters, Dirty Deeds, and Debauchery in Boston

Start: Transportation Building, at the intersection of Charles and Stuart Streets

Getting there: Take the MBTA Green Line to Boylston Street Station

Finish: The North End intersection of Commercial and Snow Hill Streets

Getting back: Take the MBTA Green Line from North Station

Time: 1½ hours

Distance: 2 miles

Difficulty: Easy

Accessibility: Fully wheelchair accessible

Rest rooms: National Park Service Headquarters on State Street opposite Old State House

---

IF YOU'VE BEEN LED to believe that Boston is steeped only in patriotism, Brahmin sensibilities, Ivory Towers, and the Kennedys—think again. All is not sugar and spice in one of America's oldest cities; the dark side is never more than a few steps away! Boston's less-than-illustrious past extends from the

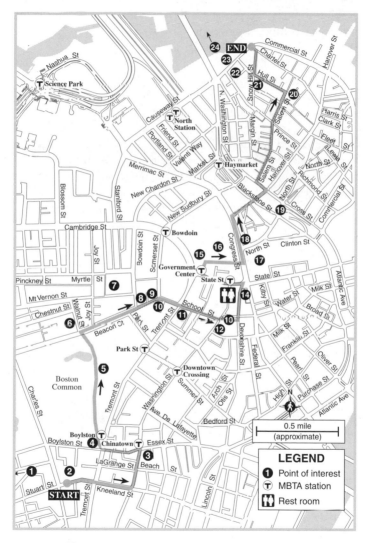

Disasters, Dirty Deeds, and Debauchery in Boston

arrival of the Puritans to the present day, with a ghastly deed lurking around every corner. As you stroll down the quaint streets of Boston, discovering its sometimes sordid past, you may look at this historic old city in an entirely new light.

This tour delivers you to a number of Boston sites that have seen their share of calamities, evil doings, and flauntings of the flesh. You'll discover where colonists were killed by red-coats at the Old State House and townsfolk in the North End died in a flood of molasses. If you're fascinated by the "Wives of Satan," old Mount Whoredom, Scollay Square, and the Combat Zone should get your attention. Or if ghosts are your bag, see if you can find the specter of a drunkard drinking his way to death, a subway rider who couldn't find his way off the MBTA, or a group of corpses displaced from their burial sites. Not merely puritanical, Boston has been the home of armed robberies, violent racial hatred, crooked politicians, and many more less-than-savory activities.

🚶 the walk

▶ **Begin in front of the Transportation Building on Stuart Street near the corner of Charles Street.**

Facing Stuart Street, look right for the *John Hancock Tower (1),* a 1973 disaster. While the sixty-story skyscraper was under construction, huge windows started popping out, raining glass onto Copley Square. The gaping window openings were temporarily replaced with plywood, giving the building the honor of being for a short time the tallest plywood-clad building in the world. ▶ **Head east on Stuart Street.**

Near the corner of Stuart and New Charles Street was the *Cocoanut Grove (2),* an infamous nightclub that burned in the most disastrous fire in Boston's history. This 1942 blaze killed 492 clubgoers in less than fifteen minutes; emergency doors were locked, and people couldn't escape. The fire led to the discovery of penicillin as a major treatment for World War II burn victims. ▶ **Continue east on Stuart Street to Washington Street and turn left.**

The *Combat Zone (3)* was Boston's notorious red-light district in the 1970s, named for its popularity with sailors and soldiers. Now a shadow of its boisterous past, the area once hosted more than thirty peep shows, X-rated movie theaters, and strip clubs. In 1974 stripper Fanne Foxe escorted U.S. congressman Wilbur Mills into the old Pilgrim Theater, creating a Washington scandal as Mills staggered onto the stage. ▶ **Turn left onto Boylston Street and walk to the corner of Tremont Street.**

Builders of the 1897 *Boylston MBTA Station (4)* found 910 colonial bodies buried here, reinterring them elsewhere. Their spirits are said to still haunt the Green Line. Speaking of spirits and personal disaster, Charlie on the MTA, commemorated by the Kingston Trio, is still riding the train, at least in song, because he couldn't afford the fare to get off. Perhaps the dirtiest Green Line deed was that of Rosie Ruiz, who in 1980 won the Boston Marathon by riding it to the finish line. ▶ **Head north across the Common.**

On Boston Common was the *Great Elm (5)*, also known as the Hanging Tree. In Puritan times Quakers, adulterers, and witches were all subject to hanging, and hanging days frequently became public holidays. ▶ **Cross Beacon Street.** Prominent physician George Parkman lived at *8 Walnut Street (6)* until 1849, when he was murdered by Harvard professor John Webster over a debt. Parkman's dismembered body, discovered in a vault under Webster's office, led to a frenzied trial—the first trial in which dental work was used as evidence. ▶ **Proceed northeast on Beacon.**

From 1962 through 1964 the Boston Strangler terrorized *Beacon Hill (7)*, strangling and sexually molesting thirteen women. Albert DiSalvo confessed to being the Strangler, was jailed, but was never tried or convicted. DNA evidence today suggests that he may have been innocent.

Just left of the State House is the *site of John Hancock's house (8)*. Rumors were that Hancock amassed a fortune by pilfering from Harvard College, where he was treasurer. Many believe that Harvard money is still buried on the State House grounds.

At the State House is a statue of *General Joseph Hooker (9)*, a Civil War general who lost most of his battles but was popular with his troops because he allowed women to follow them, thus keeping up soldier morale. The women became known as "Hookers."

Number 10 ½ Beacon, the *Boston Athenaeum (10)*, owns a human-skin-covered book. In 1833 John Fenno was shot and robbed at gunpoint by James Allen but managed to capture his assailant. In prison Allen wrote the memoirs of his life as a highway robber and in his will provided that a copy of the book, bound in his own skin, should be given to Mr. Fenno for his bravery.

At Beacon and Tremont Streets stands the *Parker House (11)*. Room 303, it is said, houses the ghost of a man who drank himself to death. Visitors to the room attest to noises, apparitions, and the lingering stench of whiskey. In another room John Wilkes Booth lodged for a week before shooting Lincoln. ❱ **Walk down School Street to Washington Street.**

In the bustle of today's downtown activity, it's difficult to imagine the *Great Fire of Boston (12)*. In 1872 a fire engulfed most of downtown, destroying 776 buildings and stopping just short of Old South Meeting House. Many horse-pulled fire engines were unable to respond because influenza had afflicted most of the city's horses. ❱ **Turn left onto Washington Street, then immediately right onto Spring Lane.**

Spring Lane (13) is site of one of Boston's earliest springs—a major source of water. For colonists, bathing twice a year was typical. The entire family usually bathed in the same water, perhaps resulting in the expression: "Don't throw out the baby with the bathwater." ❱ **Follow Devonshire Street left** to its intersection with State Street.

A sidewalk marker memoralizes the *Boston Massacre (14)*. In 1770 British soldiers, threatened by an angry mob, fired in self-defense, killing five colonists. The Brits, defended by ardent patriots John Adams and Josiah Quincy, were all acquitted. ❱ **Proceed left on State to City Hall Plaza.**

Part of the plaza is the *site of Scollay Square (15)*, known for burlesque shows and tattoo parlors popular with servicemen. The square's Old Howard Theatre featured burlesque and Sally Keith, the Tassel Queen. Ticket takers spotting city inspectors or police would flash warnings to performers on stage to clean up their acts.

When a 1970s court order mandated Boston school desegregation, *City Hall Plaza (16)* was the scene of ugly racial violence. Some white people attacked a black man with a flagpole and American flag, an image memorialized in a Pulitzer Prize–winning photograph seen all over the country.

Below City Hall is *Faneuil Hall (17)* with its gilded copper 39-pound grasshopper weathervane. In 1755 it fell off during a major earthquake (6 on the Richter scale). Replaced on its perch, it was removed by thieves in 1974, but fortunately was recovered. ❱ **Turn left at Faneuil Hall and proceed up Congress Street.**

Look for *James Michael Curley Park (18)*, honoring a great orator and "friend of the people." A three-time mayor (1914–49), a governor, and a congressman, Curley was first elected as a city alderman in 1904 while in prison for taking a postal exam for a friend. In 1946 he was elected mayor despite being indicted for mail fraud and sentenced to jail. President Truman pardoned him after five months, and Curley returned a hero. ❱ **Turn right onto Hanover Street.**

Just past Blackstone Street is the *Central Artery (19)*, where tunneling and excavations by archaeologists unearthed treasures from seventeenth-century privies. One treasure may be the oldest bowling ball found in this country. Bowling was

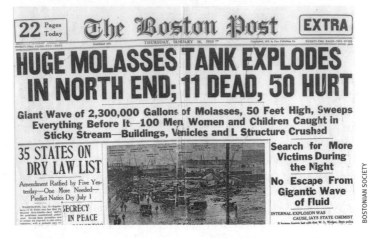

A 1919 newpaper headline.

then illegal, and the players likely had to get rid of the evidence quickly. Although the Artery project originally had a price tag of $2.5 billion, by 2002 it had spiraled into a cost disaster—more than $14 billion, with no end in sight. ▶ **Turn left onto Cross Street, then right onto Salem Street; continue to Hull Street.**

Old North Church (20) was memorialized by Longfellow in "One if by land and two if by sea." Longfellow's poem lionized Paul Revere, but William Dawes and Samuel Prescott warned more people than Revere because—unlike him—they didn't get captured. However, their names didn't rhyme with "Listen my children and you shall hear . . ." ▶ **Turn left onto Hull Street.**

Across from the cemetery is the *Spite House (21),* the narrowest house in Boston at 10 feet, built to block the light from the house behind it. ▶ **Turn right onto Snow Hill Street.**

The site of the *Brink's Robbery (22)* is now a public parking garage. In 1950 nine bandits stole $2.7 million from the garage, where the Brinks Company parked its armored trucks. Only $50,000 was ever recovered. Hundreds of local people were accessories to the crime.

Just below the garage was the *Great Molasses Flood (23)*. In 1919, with Prohibition looming, a rum distiller overfilled a molasses tank, and it burst. In a wave cresting at 30 feet and moving at 35 MPH, 2.5 million gallons of molasses drowned twenty-one people and destroyed eight buildings. Locals claim that on a hot day, they can still smell molasses. ◗ **Cross Commercial Street.**

At the river's edge, look at the *Tobin Bridge (24)*. In 1989 Charles Stuart shot and killed his pregnant wife and tried to make it look like the work of a mugger from Mission Hill. When found out, he committed suicide by "Pulling a Chuck" off the Tobin Bridge.

◗ **The walk ends here. For public transit access, follow Commercial Street to North Station.**

ERIK SCHEIER *is a project director with the Massachusetts Bay Transportation Authority and a tour guide for Boston by Foot.*

walk 2

Brookline's Secret Stairways and Paths

Start: Washington Square, Beacon and Washington Streets
Getting there: Take the MBTA Green Line C Train (Beacon Street) to Washington Square Station
Finish: Brookline Hills MBTA Station
Getting back: Take the MBTA Green Line D Train from Brookline Hills
Time: 2 hours
Distance: 2.5 miles
Difficulty: Moderate to strenuous on stairways and uphill grades
Accessibility: Many stairways and hills; not wheelchair accessible
Rest rooms: Brookline High School and Recreation Center

A PLEASURE UNIQUE to Boston is tracing the dramatic topography left by the great glacier when it passed through New England. The glacier marked the Boston Basin with a series of high hills overlooking the harbor and kettle holes where great blocks of ice were left behind to melt. Although they're now blanketed with urban development, these hills gave the town of Brookline an unusual legacy: pedestrian pathways and stairways built as links between neighborhoods.

The golden age of Brookline development began in 1890,

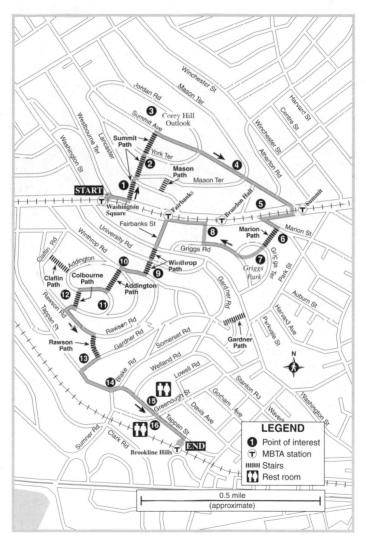

Brookline's Secret Stairways and Paths

WALKBOSTON STAFF

Marian Path, Brookline.

when a streetcar company transformed a narrow rural roadway into the 160-foot-wide Beacon Street boulevard, with
landscaping, pedestrian walkways, and tracks for streetcars
down the middle. The neighborhood was instantly stylish—
an extension of fashionable Back Bay. With easy access to

Boston via the streetcar, wealthy families built mansions along the new boulevard. Apartment hotels were added, and clusters of town houses graced side streets. The most radical features—pedestrian stairways running up and down the hillside—provided shortcuts between the hilltop and the neighborhoods and streetcars down below.

This walk focuses on two of Brookline's glaciated hills, Corey and Aspinwall. Landscape architect Frederick Law Olmsted (renowned for his design of New York's Central Park) was called in to plan the latter. His new neighborhood provided views out over the surrounding countryside, with many paths and stairways down to the valleys. Almost too good to be true, this grand design was assembled because Olmsted simply paid no attention to property lines. When his employers discovered that he'd laid out streets beyond their holdings and onto other people's property, he was summarily fired. Later, a less intrepid designer negotiated public paths along property lines on the hillside.

Today Brookline's stairways and walkways remain safe, convenient facilities that provide an energetic walk over glacial features only partially obscured by urban growth. This brief tour will show you why these hidden pedestrian corridors should no longer be a secret.

the walk

▶ **Starting at the Washington Square clock, walk east along Beacon Street toward Boston. Look for a street sign between 1592 and 1600 Beacon Street marking the beginning of Summit Path.**

On the left at 1600 Beacon is the site of the *Jordan mansion "Stonehurst" (1).* Built in 1890, this was the home of Eben Jordan, heir to a cofounder of the Jordan Marsh Department Store (now Macy's). When his father died, Eben Junior moved to Boston to mind the family retail business. He helped establish the Boston Opera House and the New England Conservatory of Music, where the performance space named Jordan Hall still honors him. The Brookline Jordan house, used as the Choate School until 1947, adjoined the now demolished home of King Gillette, founder of the razor firm. ❱ **Turn left onto Summit Path.**

Summit Path (2) ascends Corey Hill, which Jordan developed as a residential community. Three parallel streets ring the hill in terraces from bottom to top. To accommodate transportation needs of hill residents, Jordan built these steps and slopes from the hill to the streetcar stop and stores on Beacon Street. ❱ **At the top of the hill, turn left for a short distance to a small park.**

Corey Hilltop Park (3) overlooks the city. Each Sunday in the mid–nineteenth century hundreds of people would climb this hill to view a broad rural panorama, from the distant peaks of Monadnock and Wachusett Mountains to the islands of Boston Harbor. The hilltop was said to be four to six degrees warmer in winter than the valleys below, and cooler in summer. Until the late nineteenth century Corey Hill provided winter toboggan runs for children and spring and fall camps for gypsies in the fields. ❱ **Proceed southeast down Summit Avenue (4).**

This street was paved in the 1860s, with "a plank walk laid out for pedestrians." In contrast to nearby terraced streets, Summit is very steep and runs straight down the hill.

At the bottom of the hill along Beacon Street are one-story *"Taxpayer Buildings" (5)* that replaced mansions lining the boulevard. Intended to be temporary, they were rented to retail outlets to provide income, allowing landowners to pay taxes while they waited for an opportunity to build a multi-storied and profitable apartment building. Now a permanent part of the town, the buildings are preserved as part of the Beacon Street Historic District. ❱ **Turn left onto Marion Street.**

Narrow and shaded, *Marion Path (6)*, to the right, leads off Marion Street to the Griggs Park community. Marion Path's gradual slope saves area residents many steps on a shortcut route better than sidewalks on nearby roads. Beacon Street residents use the path for access to the playground and the park.

Water-loving willows are a reminder that *Griggs Park (7)* is a marshy kettle hole formed by a chunk of ice left behind by a primeval glacier. A quiet oasis in a densely built neighborhood, the park is a playground for all ages, with a water area for frogs and birds in the forested center. The narrow two-way roadway that surrounds the park encourages motorists to drive slowly and carefully. ❱ **Leaving Griggs Park, turn right onto Griggs Road and then right again onto a narrow private street leading to the high-rise at 1500 Beacon Street.**

Brandon Hall (8) was a 1904 apartment hotel that some considered the center of fashionable suburban Brookline because of its lavish beauty and ease of transit access. Though destroyed by fire, its name remains on the streetcar stop. ❱ **Turn left onto Beacon Street and left again at Fairbanks Street. Jog right at the top of Winthrop Path (9) to reach Addington Path (10).**

The climb up Aspinwall Hill was initially planned as a grand design to connect a Beacon Street transit stop to the hilltop; Winthrop and Addington Paths still reflect this plan. Boston University nearly located its campus on Aspinwall Hill in the nineteenth century. When it lost many properties in the Great Fire of 1872 in downtown Boston, however, BU sold its Brookline land to recoup its losses.

On Aspinwall Hilltop, Addington Road surrounds *Schick Park (11)*, a 1945 facility that replaced a Bavarian-style castle/mansion perched at the top of the hill. Zigzagging Aspinwall Hill streets encouraged developers to build *Colbourne Path (12)* as a shortcut down the west side of Aspinwall Hill. ❱ **At the bottom of Colbourne Path, cross**

Rawson Road and look for the path sign between Nos. 114 and 120–124 Rawson Road. *Rawson Path (13)* is another shortcut, a step-saving, steep, and heavily wooded walkway down Aspinwall Hill leading to Gardner Road. ❱ **Turn right onto Gardner, then left onto Tappan Street.**

The large Blake estate became *Blake Park (14),* a residential neighborhood, in the 1920s. Streets were laid out on earlier paths on the nineteenth-century estate. Royal Barry Wills, the designer of twenty-seven of these Colonial-style houses, won the 1932 Better Homes in America competition for one of the designs. Examples of Wills-designed homes may be seen on Blake Road.

Brookline High School (15) and, across the street, the *Brookline Recreation Center (16)* both house rest rooms. ❱ **The walk ends at the nearby Brookline Hills MBTA Station.**

ROBERT SLOANE, *a Brookline resident, lawyer, and city planner, serves as Walks Chair for WalkBoston.*

 **walk 3**

The Fields of Newton

Start: MBTA Newton Centre Station
Getting there: Take the MBTA Green Line D Train to
   Newton Centre
Finish: MBTA Lake Street Station
Getting back: Take the MBTA Green Line B Train from
   Lake Street
Time: 3 hours
Distance: 4 miles
Difficulty: Hilly, walkable surfaces
Accessibility: Fully wheelchair accessible
Rest rooms: McElroy Commons, at the corner of College
   Road and Beacon Street; BC Law School

IMAGINING FIELDS in today's Newton takes a giant leap of
faith. Yet it is possible for a sensitive walker to trace the
underlying structure of the community by exploring its
topography, its oldest roads, and the residential buildings that
uniformly blanket the area. You can find vestiges of the old
fields in open land and in the spacious settings of institutions
built on large parcels.

Not that long ago, however, Newton consisted entirely of
fields, farms, and grazing pastures. Flat or gently rolling
topography and relatively fertile soil kept farming attractive

here for more than two hundred years. Rocky or hilly areas that could not be made into fields became woodlots for timber growing and harvesting.

When the railroad arrived and commuting began in about 1850, however, rows of housing took the place of many of the fields. Today the development of Newton's fields can often be dated by examining variants of architectural styles. Indeed, this walk is a virtual primer on residential architecture: you'll pass styles ranging from Stick to Colonial to Queen Anne to Shingle.

In its search for the remnants of Newton's long-ago fields, this walk begins at Newton Centre Station and the railroad that was the chief driving force bringing people to Newton. You'll trace the city's remaining open lands and parks and explore the old farmland that now hosts educational or ecclesiastical institutions. Along the way you'll have the chance to spot homes from fanciful to puritanical.

🚶 the walk

The railroads that changed Newton into its present form are magnificently evident in the *Newton Centre Railroad Station (1)*, this walk's starting point. The terminal was designed by prominent architect H. H. Richardson and completed by his successor firm, Shepley, Rutan & Coolidge, in 1890. Romanesque in style, it boasts rough-hewn stone-block construction with contrasting coloration. Built to serve commuters on the Boston & Albany rail line to Boston, the station is owned by the MBTA. ▶ **Follow Union Path northwest to reach Beacon Street.**

The old *Newton Centre Common (2)* occupied the present triangular area now surrounded by shops. The flatness of the terrain suggests one of its early uses, as a colonial militia training field. Structures here once included a powderhouse and two "noon-houses"—places where communal midday

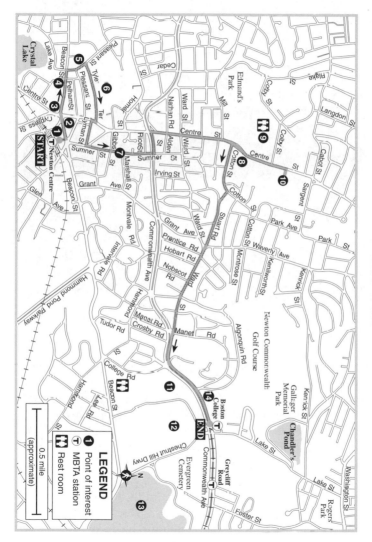

The Fields of Newton

BOB BERGMAN, MARKETING IMAGES

MBTA Station, Newton Centre.

Sunday meals were served to parishioners who lived far from the nearby meetinghouse. At the corner of the common is a horse- and dog-watering trough (now a flower planter). ▶ **Cross Centre Street to proceed west on Beacon Street.**

To the left, the *First Baptist Church (3)* was built in 1888 in the Richardsonian Romanesque style. Its octagonal belfry features an impressive array of hewn- and carved-stone elements. Farther down the street, one of Newton's best examples of a *Stick-style house (4)* is found at 908 Beacon, with large half-timbers, heavy porch bracing, and a central tower with a pyramidal roof. ▶ **Turn right onto Lake Avenue.**

At the corner of Lake and Pleasant Street is a row of sev-

eral *Gothic cottages (5)* built in the 1860s on a large piece of
land. Note the scalloped bargeboards and flattened arches
surrounding bracketed front bays. ◗ **Turn right onto Tyler
Terrace.**

The *Newton Centre Playground (6),* in a large field to the
left, resulted when the Newton Centre Improvement Association hired the renowned Frederick Law Olmsted and his
firm to lay out playing fields. The Recreation Hut at the edge
of the park is the former Trinity Church. ◗ **Cross Centre
Street carefully and proceed down Lyman Street. At Sumner
Street, turn left.**

Sumner Street (7) has one of the best collections of
Victorian residential architecture in the city. The variety of
housing may be seen in examples of the Shingle style (120
and 180 Sumner), Stick style (147 and 166), Queen Anne
style (126, 140, and 156), Colonial Revival (105, 106, 134,
and 155), and Second Empire/mansard style (131 and 139).
◗ **Follow Sumner to Commonwealth Avenue and turn left,
then right onto Centre Street.**

At Cotton and Centre Streets is the *Old Burying Ground
(8),* site of Newton's first meetinghouse and cemetery (1660).
Today the First Settlers' Monument, erected in 1852, marks
this historic location.

Beyond the cemetery both sides of Centre Street are lined
with open areas that focus on institutions. On the left is the
Boston College Law School (9), which moved in 1974 to this
leafy campus, once the Newton College of the Sacred Heart.
On the right, *Carroll Center for the Blind (10),* established in
1936, sits amid gently rolling fields that convey the feeling of
open farmland. ◗ **Retrace your steps to Cotton Street and
turn left. Cotton Street turns into Stuart Road and then
Ward Street.**

As you proceed down Ward Street, look for several
eighteenth-century homes tucked between more modern
buildings. The path reaches *Boston College (11)* on the upper

roadway parallel to Commonwealth Avenue. BC occupies a large tract that was once the Lawrence farm (named for industrialist Amos Lawrence). Founded in 1863, the college originally opened in Boston's South End and began its move to the large farm's fields in 1909.

Turn right down Chestnut Hill Driveway to view the *college playing fields (12),* given to the institution in 1950 and now the site of the Boston College Stadium. Just beyond is the *Chestnut Hill Reservoir (13),* an artificial pond created on flat fields in 1875 to store water for Boston. ◗ **Return to Commonwealth Avenue.**

On the right, farther toward Boston, the *residence of the archbishop of the Boston Roman Catholic Archdiocese* and the *St. John's Seminary (14)* are set in a large open area. The land was purchased with funds from Benjamin F. Keith, a theater owner, who died in 1918 and left a bequest of $2 million. An Italian Renaissance chancery was erected in 1926; the present chancery was added in the 1960s. Nearby, on Lake Street, St. John's Seminary occupies buildings of Roxbury puddingstone quarried from the site.

◗ **The walk concludes at the intersection of Lake Street and Commonwealth Avenue, with access to the Green Line.**

SHARON TRAMER, *a clinical research technologist at McLean Hospital in Belmont, has been active with peace and earth-preservation groups for the past twenty-five years.*

 **walk 4**

The Hills of Somerville

Start and finish: Davis Square
Getting there: Take the MBTA Red Line to Davis Square
Getting back: Return on the MBTA Red Line
Time: 3.5 hours
Distance: 4 miles
Difficulty: Several uphill (and downhill) hikes
Accessibility: Fully wheelchair accessible
Rest rooms: Somerville Museum; Somerville City Hall

LIKE AN EAST COAST San Francisco, Somerville's street grid is imposed on its hills without regard to steep grades. Architects have capitalized on the city's resulting dramatic views with two- and three-family houses densely built in straight rows climbing the hills. This unusual loop walk through the city's heart takes in many of its cultural, historical, and architectural landmarks.

The city's glacial hills and deep valleys were first settled by colonial farmers. Their roads—which followed crests or valleys—still exist in the form of modern-day Broadway, Somerville Avenue, Elm Street, Main Street, Washington Street, and others.

Farmers' lands were parceled out perpendicular to the roads, with crude paths or lanes every quarter mile. These lanes, or rangeways, are now the city's crosstown streets. The curious street grid may have helped guide the later grid layout of the Midwest and western parts of the country, including, of course, San Francisco.

Early development followed the colonial roads; the unpaved rangeways were too hilly for regular horseback or carriage traffic. In the nineteenth century railroads, thoroughfares, and streetcars were all laid out along this skeleton as well, allowing Somerville to become both an industrial center and, at one point, the most densely populated city in the country.

The city retains much of the character of its past. The hills still undulate beneath the densely developed residential community. Travel on the main streets is smooth, but it is more difficult on the crosstown streets. From the leafy hilltops, there are frequent views overlooking the surrounding city.

This walk gives an overview of Somerville, following its early streets, taking in its rich history—including many sites pivotal in the American Revolution—and looking at the influence of topography and transportation lines that molded the residential areas. It is, as you'll see, a remarkable city.

🚶 the walk

The walk begins at *Davis Square (1)*, originally a sharp bend in the old colonial road. After 1860 horse-drawn streetcar lines and then a steam railroad were built. Residential and commercial development followed. Rail passenger service stopped in the 1920s, and the line became a freight-only route; as recently as 1979 long freight trains rumbled across the square in the middle of the night.

The Red Line subway was built on the route of the old freight trains in 1984. Since then Davis Square has prospered and become an attractive destination. A highlight of the square is the *Somerville Theatre (2)*, erected in 1914 for vaude-

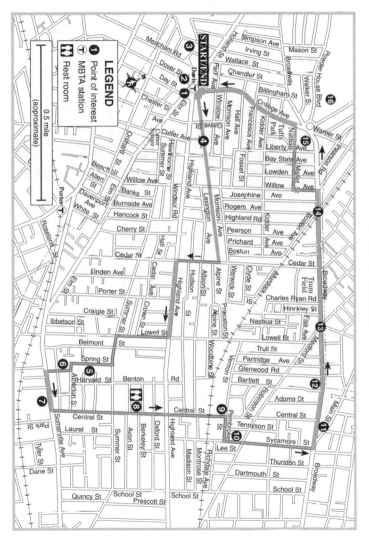

The Hills of Somerville

ville and motion pictures and now a very active community performance center and cinema.

Two pathways follow the former railroad land. To the west is *Linear Park (3),* built atop the subway as a connection to the Minuteman Rail-Trail at Alewife. Just west of the subway station is Seven Hills Park, where you can see the *Hills of Somerville*—sculptures on poles lining the path.

To the east is the *Community Path (4),* a 1997 continuation of Linear Park. ❱ **To reach the start of the Community Path, follow the sidewalk next to the busway beside the College Avenue subway entrance, then continue straight through the parking lot.** Willow Avenue is the first of the seventeenth-century rangeways this walk will intersect; from here you'll encounter them every quarter mile. At Hancock Street a playground occupies the site of the Somerville Highlands Railroad Station.

The Community Path currently ends at Cedar Street (another rangeway), but there are plans to extend it farther, possibly to Lechmere Square in Cambridge. ❱ **Turn right onto Cedar Street, then left onto Highland Avenue, and begin to climb.** This is Spring Hill, an elongated ridge extending across the city. ❱ **Turn right onto Lowell Street; left onto Summer Street; and right onto Spring Street.**

At Spring Street you enter the *Spring Hill Historic District (5).* From the top of the hill, note the view of Harvard University buildings in the distance. At the corner of Atherton Street is the unusual *Round House (6).* The 40-foot-diameter house, built in 1856, features a glass-domed central hall surrounded by circular and oval rooms. It was built during a period of experimentation with octagonal and other nearly round housing types. The 40-foot-diameter house reflected the builder's hope that he could remove the devil from the corners of a house by simply removing the corners. ❱ **Follow Spring Street to the bottom of the hill and turn left.**

Somerville Avenue (7) was the route used by the British sol-

Old Powder House, Nathan Tufts Park, Somerville.

diers on their fateful trek to Concord and Lexington. Across the street, Conway Park was built on reclaimed industrial land. ▶ **Turn left onto Central Street and proceed uphill through more of the Spring Hill Historic District.**

The *Somerville Museum (8)*, at the corner of Westwood Road, proudly displays the original doors, mantels, and a grand stairway from a mansion built in 1793 by architect Charles Bulfinch, who also designed the Boston State House. The mansion, built for the Barrell family in East Somerville, became the first McLean Hospital. (Call 617-666-9810 for hours.)

At Highland Avenue the city hall, high school, and public library are visible crowning a hill a quarter mile to the right. ❚ **Continue straight downhill on Central Street.** As you cross the bridge, you can see the old Somerville junction of the railroad. Look to the left for the split of the still-used main line from the branch that became the Community Path. Adjacent to the bridge is a huge *Victorian factory (9)* where rolltop desks were once made; it now hosts both manufacturing and artists' studios. ❚ **Divert to the right on Pembroke Street for two short blocks, then turn left onto Sycamore Street.**

At 78 Sycamore is the oldest house in Somerville: the *Oliver Tufts House (10),* built in 1714 in the middle of a farm. The gambrel-roofed structure was headquarters for General Charles Lee of the Continental army during the siege of Boston in 1775–76. ❚ **Follow Sycamore Street to Broadway and turn left.** If you look to the right before you turn, you'll see an expansive view down Broadway culminating in the Bunker Hill Monument in the distance.

You are nearing the crest of the highest and longest hill in Somerville, Winter Hill, extending some 4,000 feet from East Somerville toward Medford. One of the city's major business districts extends down the hill toward Charlestown. Nearby Marshall Street was once the headquarters of the notorious Winter Hill gang of organized crime.

Soon Broadway branches, with Main Street leading off to the right. The latter was the old Winter Hill Road, the route of Paul Revere as he rode on April 19, 1775. His ride is commemorated by the tiny *Paul Revere Park (11)* in the middle of the fork.

At 438 Broadway you'll see Somerville's second oldest residence, the *Adams-Magoun House (12)*, a circa-1783 farm-house with a Federal-period front door. Notice the two-level street, with a service road accessing the abutting buildings. Going down the hill you come to *Magoun Square (13)*, a six-legged street intersection with a small commercial area. In colonial times this area was the Magoun family farm. A few blocks beyond is *Ball Square (14)*, with shops serving students at nearby Tufts University. ❱ **Leave Broadway by turning left onto Willow Avenue and then right onto Mallet Street, until you come to Nathan Tufts Park.** Here is the *Old Powder House (15)*, an early-eighteenth-century windmill that ground grain until it became a storehouse for gunpowder in 1747. The round granite-and-slate structure on old Quarry Hill was the site of a 1774 incursion by the redcoats, who seized 250 half barrels of powder stored here in one of the first hostile acts of the Revolution.

From the park you can view the main campus of *Tufts University (16)*. Beyond Powder House Square, the principal college buildings can be seen crowning College Hill. Tufts, founded in 1852, is worth a stroll if you have time. Look for the hilltop College Green, and the President's Lawn just off Professors Row. ❱ **Turn left and follow College Avenue southwest away from Tufts.**

Just past the park, look left on Francesca Avenue, with its undulating surfaces. Continue down College Avenue past spired churches and multifamily buildings to return to Davis Square.

❱ **The walk ends at Davis Square.**

CHARLES BAHNE *is a Boston historian.*

 **walk 5**

Boston's South Bay and the Shirley-Eustis House

Start and finish: Andrew Square in South Boston at the corner of Dorchester Avenue and Southampton, Boston, Preble, and Dorchester Streets
Getting there: Take the MBTA Red Line to Andrew Station
Getting back: Return on the MBTA Red Line
Time: 2 hours (without a tour of the Shirley-Eustis House)
Distance: Approximately 3 miles
Difficulty: Easy
Accessibility: Fully wheelchair accessible
Rest rooms: Shirley-Eustis House (during opening hours)

THIS WALK LEADS you through the modern bustle of South Bay and environs—yet if you look past the energy of modern commerce with some imagination, you can still visualize three-masted sailing ships, muscular steam locomotives, aristocratic estates, horse-drawn streetcars, scientific agriculture, and personalities of an earlier age who shaped and were shaped by the evolution of this area.

When the Puritans arrived in Boston, they found two large bays separated by a narrow sandbar isthmus roughly following today's Washington Street. The northern bay abutting the Charles River was called Back Bay. The southern bay—

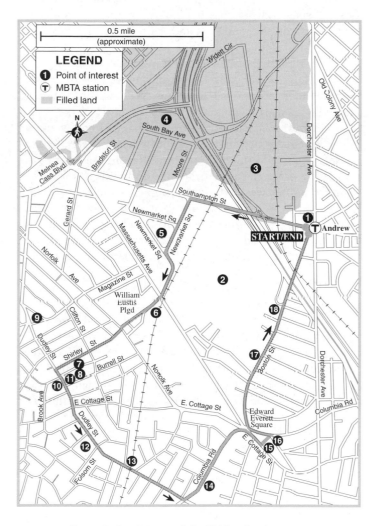

Boston's South Bay and the Shirley-Eustis House

unsurprisingly named South Bay—was a large tidal marsh. While stout piers and deepwater wharves lined the busy Boston waterfront, in the two bays early settlers conducted weir fishing on the mud flats and gathered salt hay from the meadows for animal feed, much as indigenous peoples had since the beginning of human habitation.

The bluffs overlooking South Bay, graced by the stately mansion of British royal governor William Shirley, were gradually lined with homes by the local gentry of the young republic. But the bucolic bay they looked out upon would be radically transformed by the advent of steam power. Massachusetts emerged from the American Revolution just in time for the Industrial Revolution, and the economic history of the young republic was writ large: higher population, bigger homes, larger ships, and expansive wharves. Over the nineteenth century these forces transformed the two bays utterly: Back Bay was filled in for homes, churches, colleges, and museums, while South Bay was devoted to industry and commerce.

Oddly, the first change that South Bay saw was an enlargement: in the 1830s the bay was expanded to the south as dirt from the shore was barged to the north side and used as fill for Boston's first railroad yards. Immediately thereafter the process of filling the bay for industry began—a process that would continue well into the twentieth century. Finally, in the 1950s, the Southeast Expressway was built through the area. Today only the Fort Point Channel remains as a reminder of South Bay's watery history. This walk lets you explore today's South "Bay," the neighborhood that landfill built.

the walk

The walk begins at *Andrew Square (1)* upstairs from the MBTA Andrew Red Line Station. The square is named in honor of Governor John Andrew, who raised the famous

Fifty-fourth Massachusetts Regiment of Free Negroes during the Civil War. ❱ **Walk west on Southampton Street.** Your route travels over the Old Colony Railroad branch and Southeast Expressway, providing good overviews of the next sites.

The *South Bay Shopping Center (2)* was the tidal salt meadow that was dug out in the 1830s to provide fill for Boston's first railyards on the other side of the bay. This area remained open water until after World War I.

Much of the filled-in South Bay now serves as the *Amtrak and MBTA railroad yards (3)*. In 1846 the Old Colony Railroad—named for the earlier 1620 Plymouth Colony—was built from Boston to Plymouth. The line was initially routed down today's Old Colony Avenue but was relocated and new yards added on South Bay landfill shortly before World War I. ❱ **Continue west on Southampton Street, passing under a railroad line, and turn left at the first opportunity.**

Before your turn you can see the *Suffolk County House of Correction (4)*, a high-rise with small windows. This site hosted the last oceangoing ship wharf before the Southeast Expressway was built in the 1950s and the filling of South Bay was completed.

Construction of the expressway provided improved truck access, and businesses from Quincy Market relocated in the area called *Newmarket (5)*. This accelerated Quincy Market's decline prior to becoming a textbook case of adaptive reuse in the 1970s. ❱ **Cross Massachusetts Avenue and continue south on Shirley Street.**

The *Victoria Dining parking lot (6)* sits on what was the southernmost open water after South Bay was enlarged. Salt meadow extended farther south to the bluffs.

Rising from the former salt meadow onto the bluff is the *Shirley-Eustis House (7)*, the mansion built in 1747 by Governor William Shirley. (You will approach the home from the rear.) William Eustis purchased it in 1819 upon his

SHIRLEY-EUSTIS HOUSE ASSOCIATION

The 1774 Shirley-Eustis House.

return from serving as ambassador to the Netherlands. The house is furnished in the Empire-style decor that Eustis brought back from Europe. Eustis, elected governor in 1824, died in office the following year. His widow, Caroline Langdon Eustis (daughter of Governor Langdon of New Hampshire), lived here until her death in 1865. Guided tours are available June through September, Thursday through Sunday noon–4 (or by arrangement). The cost is $5 ($3 for seniors and children). Call (617) 442-2275 or visit www. shirleyeustishouse.org.

The grounds of the *Shirley-Eustis House (8)* are always open for public enjoyment. The 1806 Ingersoll-Gardner Carriage House, moved from Brookline, was reconstructed here in 2001. A historic orchard is being cultivated to illustrate the importance of pomology (the science and practice of fruit growing) in Roxbury prior to the Civil War. Caroline Eustis and her neighbor, Dr. Enoch Bartlett (who developed the Bartlett pear), were founding members of the Massachusetts Horticultural Society. Dr. Bartlett's home was nearby, where *St. Patrick's Church (9)* now stands.

Dorchester Brook once ran where *Rockford Street* and *Brook Avenue (10)* are today. This was the boundary between Roxbury and Dorchester from 1630 until these municipalities were annexed to Boston after the Civil War. ◗ **Turn left onto Dudley Street.**

In 1856 the city of Roxbury granted a franchise to the Metropolitan Railroad to build horse-drawn streetcar lines in Roxbury. The *Mount Pleasant carhouse and stables (11)* were located at 504 Dudley Street and the building next door (formerly three floors), respectively. In 1892 the line was converted to electric trolleys, and in 1895 operations were moved to larger facilities elsewhere.

Look on the right for the *site of Captain James Swan's mansion (12)*. One of the more colorful members of the local gentry, Swan made a fortune trading with revolutionary France, the pariah state of his day. In 1796 Swan hired Charles Bulfinch to design a brick mansion for this site. The mansion was demolished during the Great Depression and is now a public playground. Several of Swan's French objets d'art are on display at the Shirley-Eustis House.

Farther down Dudley Street, *Uphams Corner (13)* is a major commercial area serving Dorchester. From the Uphams Corner Railroad Station, hourly weekday train service to South Station provides a great view of South Bay infrastructure for the cost of only a subway fare. ◗ **At Columbia Road, proceed left.**

Old Dorchester burial ground (14), Dorchester's first, was used for almost two centuries. Dorchester was organized in 1630, the same year as Boston, Roxbury, Watertown, and the Massachusetts Bay Colony itself. ◗ **The next major intersection is Edward Everett Square; a narrow park lies at the right.**

In this park is a *statue of Governor Edward Everett (15)*. This famed orator, born near this site, also served as president of Harvard College. He is remembered today for the grand two-hour oration he delivered at Gettysburg prior to Lincoln's three-minute address.

The oldest building in today's Boston, *Blake House (16)* dates to about 1650 and is noteworthy in preservation history in that it was an early attempt to preserve a private dwelling rather than a civic structure. It was moved to this site in 1896. ❯ **Continue north from the park on Boston Street.**

Another historic structure is *Lemuel Clapp House (17),* built by Roger Clapp in 1710 and enlarged by his son Lemuel, a tanner, in 1767. "Clapp's Favorite" pear, still commercially grown, was developed here in 1820. The Dorchester Historical Society (617-295-7802) owns Blake and Clapp Houses and has a visitor program.

Originally a narrow isthmus between South and Dorchester Bays, *Dorchester Neck (18)* was a critical link in an early Revolutionary War triumph. In early 1776 cannon seized by colonial forces at Fort Ticonderoga, New York, were dragged over the snowy Berkshires and down this route under the direction of General Henry Knox. Once they were placed on Dorchester Heights in today's South Boston, General Washington was able to force the British to evacuate Boston—his first victory. ❯ **Follow Knox's cannon down Boston Street, over the expressway, and back to Andrew Square, the end of this walk.** The cannon kept going up the hill, and, as they say, the rest is history.

WILLIAM KUTTNER *serves on the Shirley-Eustis House Association board and is a transportation planner for the Boston Metropolitan Planning Organization.*

 **walk 6**

Boston's Washington Street

Start: New England Medical Center Station, MBTA Orange or Silver Line
Getting there: Take the MBTA Orange Line or Silver Line
Finish: Dudley MBTA Station
Getting back: Take the MBTA Silver Line from Dudley Station to New England Medical Center Station
Time: 2 hours
Distance: 3 miles
Difficulty: Easy
Accessibility: Fully wheelchair accessible
Rest rooms: South End Health Center

FROM DUDLEY SQUARE to Chinatown, Washington Street is in the midst of an astonishing small-business and real-estate revival that is bringing new life and vitality to this historic part of the city.

This is not, of course, the first time the area has seen enormous change. In colonial times Washington Street was a narrow land bridge connecting Boston proper, which lay out on a peninsula, to the mainland behind. Called Boston Neck and no more than 100 feet wide at some points, the bridge was surrounded by swampy marshland; when tides were very high it almost disappeared.

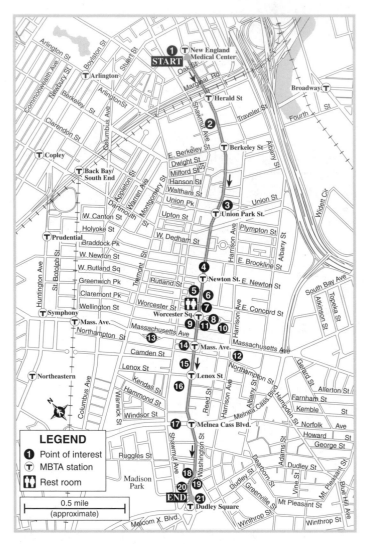

Boston's Washington Street

Over time docks began to edge the Neck; eventually a new harbor-bound railroad crossed both marsh and peninsula. When the early nineteenth century saw overcrowding of the city's center, city business and government leaders began to fill marshland along both sides of the Neck. New Chinese immigrants quickly settled near the train station at the northern edge of the filled land; farther south, wealthy merchants built elegant town houses. Then the financial panic of the 1870s led to the exodus of wealthy families; owners subdivided homes and rented to immigrants. Residents predicted that Washington Street would regain its beauty and attractiveness for development.

It took longer than they may have thought. The "El," or elevated rapid transit train, was constructed down the center of Washington Street in 1899—doing little to enhance the area's appeal. When the El was dismantled in the 1980s, however, the stage for redevelopment was finally set. Now, for the first time in nearly a hundred years, the broad thoroughfare again stands open and visible as the center of the neighborhood. Come take a stroll through one of Boston's oldest—and yet newest neighborhoods.

🚶 the walk

▶ **This walk begins at the New England Medical Center (1) and proceeds southwest on Washington Street to Dudley Square.** The medical center is surrounded by Chinatown, which extends south for several blocks.

The 1845 *Church of the Holy Trinity (2)* turns its back toward Washington Street. Successors of the original German-Catholic congregation savor the rich, full sounds of its renowned Hook and Hastings organ. The church, designed by architect John H. Keely, lost its steeple in the hurricane of 1938. A bit further along, at Berkeley Street, is the

Community Garden, founded by Chinese and Lebanese residents of the area. ❱ **Continue down Washington.**

To the right, the Morse Fish Company has sold seafood since 1903. Between Berkeley and Waltham Streets you can see a part of the area's intense development ($400 million in private and public funds) of new and renovated housing and business locations. Well over half of the new housing units will go to low- and moderate-income owner-occupants. On Harrison Avenue, one block to the left, the huge old buildings of the Warehouse District provide housing and shops for artists. Nearby is the stately old MBTA car barn between Waltham and Savoy Streets.

The 1875 *Cathedral of the Holy Cross (3),* a Gothic structure built of Roxbury puddingstone, accommodates 3,500 seated or 7,000 standing parishioners. The initial congregation, largely Irish, came to the South End in great numbers to settle in converted homes left behind by wealthy families. The yellow brick Cathedral Public Housing next door was built in 1951 and welcomed war veterans. ❱ **Cross Brookline Street.**

Blackstone and Franklin Squares (4), built in 1849, were showplace settings for residences and nearby hotels for the wealthy. Their original fountains still bubble. Alexander Graham Bell lived nearby at 35 West Newton Street, while President Ulysses Grant stayed at the Hotel St. James during the 1876 U.S. centennial celebrations. Today the hotel is Franklin Square House, an apartment building.

The South End Land Trust manages the *community garden (5)* at Washington and Rutland Streets, on land where buildings were razed under a 1960s urban renewal program. Behind the garden is one of two remaining wooden houses in the South End, dating to the 1830s. Nearby is the South End Community Health Center, a valued community resource since 1969, serving Latino families in need of local, bilingual care and preventive medicine.

On the left, the *South End Burial Ground (6)* holds, among

others, pirates and criminals executed at the nearby colonial gallows. Many of the eleven thousand people buried here could not afford tombstones. Bodies were buried aboveground in case of flooding.

The *Allen House (7)*, at 1682 Washington Street, is freestanding, unusual for the South End. It was built in 1859 in a mixture of Italianate and Second Empire architecture, with corner quoins and Moorish windows. By 1894 it housed the Catholic Union of Boston—a social club—which added a bowling alley in the basement and an auditorium.

Just behind the Allen House, *Worcester Square (8)*, a charming residential square lined with redbrick row houses, dates to the mid-1850s. Across the street at 1721–1735 Washington Street, the 1859 *Minot Hall (9)* had a 22-foot-high ballroom and grand gilded mirrors. In 1899 it was the Hotel Olympia. Damaged by fires in the 1980s, the building has been restored.

In 1908 Dr. Cornelius Garland opened *Plymouth Hospital (10)* at 12 East Springfield to train African American nurses who could not participate in Boston City Hospital's medical training and to treat a growing black population. The hospital closed in 1928 when Boston City opened its doors to African Americans.

Constructed in 1806, the *William Porter House (11)*, a Federal home at Washington and East Springfield Streets, is the oldest house in the South End on its original site. A bar in the 1960s, it is now five condominiums.

At the corner of Massachusetts Avenue, look to the left for the *Boston Medical Center (12)* with its walkway over Massachusetts Avenue. Its predecessor, Boston City Hospital, was founded in 1864 to meet a desperate need for local health care. It merged with the Boston University Medical Center in 1995 to become the present center.

A block to the right of Washington Street is *Chester Square (13)*, the largest square in the South End before Massachusetts

Avenue was built through it in the 1950s. On the square, at 558 Massachusetts Avenue, is the League of Women for Community Service, formed to assist African American soldiers during World War I. It later operated a soup kitchen, reading room, lunch programs, and housing for African American women barred from living in university dorms. In the 1850s, the house was a stop on the Underground Railroad as well, sheltering fugitive slaves on their journey to freedom.

At the right-hand corner of Massachusetts Avenue is the former *Alexandra Hotel (14)*, constructed in 1875–76, with a colorful exterior pattern in brownstone. Many prominent socialites were residents.

The *Hattie Cooper Community Center (15)*, 1891 Washington Street, was founded in 1916 during the settlement house movement to offer services to children. The mid-1970s *Ramsay Park (16)* holds Jim Rice Field, honoring the famous Boston Red Sox player. The nearby 1935 Lenox public housing was the first built for Boston's black families. Streets are named for prominent black Bostonians: Dr. Andrew Lattimore, Civil War veteran Edward A. Ditmus, and William Monroe Trotter, founder of the *Guardian. Melnea Cass Boulevard (17)* honors a black activist who worked for more than sixty years on projects ranging from suffrage for black women in the 1920s, to school desegregation in the 1960s, to labor rights for domestic workers in the 1970s.

The colorful *El Plantanero mural (18)* on the side of the Tropical Foods store reflects the international community of Roxbury. ◗ **Cross Washington Street to Eustis Street.**

Three sites make up the *Eustis Street Architectural Conservation District (19)*. The 1630 Eliot Burying Ground was the first Roxbury graveyard. Beyond it, at 20 Eustis Street, is the 1859 Eustis Street Fire Station, the oldest firehouse in the city. On Washington Street at the Burying Ground is the Owen Nawn Shop—in 1815 a soap factory, and later a tannery. ▶ **Walk along Washington Street to the right of the triangular building**.

Youth Build Boston constructed the *Dudley Heritage Wall (20)* at 2278–2286 Washington Street, a mural on the side of Ferdinand's Blue Store, a former furniture dealer.

Busy *Dudley Station (21)* opened in 1901 as the southern terminus of the Boston Elevated Railway. In 1987, after the removal of the El, the old station was converted to a bus terminal. It's now the city's largest, serving more than 30,000 passengers a day.

▶ **Catch the Silver Line back to downtown Boston.**

KIM ALLEYNE *is the manager of information and research practice at MYTOWN (Multicultural Youth Tour of What's Now).*

Part II

Exploring the Neighborhoods of Boston

 **walk 7**

Charlestown

Start: Charlestown Navy Yard, from either the Long Wharf Ferry Terminal near the MBTA Blue Line Aquarium Station or North Station on the MBTA Orange and Green Lines

Getting there: Take the ferry from Long Wharf to Charlestown Navy Yard, or walk from North Station

Finish: Sullivan Square Station on the MBTA Orange Line

Getting back: Take the MBTA Orange Line

Time: 2½ hours

Distance: Approximately 3.5 miles

Difficulty: Moderate to strenuous; the climb up Bunker Hill Monument and the steps at Forty Flights can be omitted

Accessibility: Fully wheelchair accessible

Rest rooms: At the Navy Yard's Drydock 2, Constitution Museum, and National Park Visitors Center; at the Bunker Hill Monument

---

CHARLESTOWN is Boston's oldest neighborhood—and over the years has been arguably its most volatile. This single square mile of turf bred and witnessed conflicts almost from the arrival of European settlers. For centuries the town trained and outfitted the nation's military forces; it has seen ethnic, racial, and labor tensions simmer and erupt into violence; it has hosted one of history's most infamous executions.

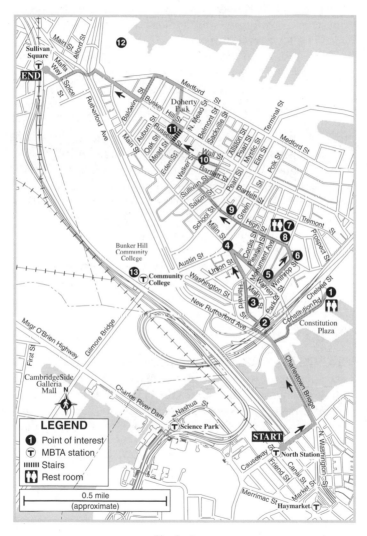

Charlestown

And that's not even to mention Charlestown's two high points (literally!): Bunker Hill (where the first battle of the American Revolution was supposed to take place) and Breed's Hill (where it did).

These days Charlestown is perhaps more serene, yet no less fascinating. This walk takes you through the town's compact heart and past its most colorful and historic sites. You'll also take in architecture from the Federal period to the present, dramatic topography with stunning views of city and harbor, and national landmarks such as the Bunker Hill Monument and the USS *Constitution.* Charlestown's streetscape, designed in the seventeenth century, remains walker-friendly. Its residents are amazingly diverse—descendants of Yankee, Irish, Italian, Portuguese, and French Canadian immigrants along with more recent Asian, African American, and Latin American immigrants and young urban professionals. And consider concluding your stroll with a stop at any of the town's myriad excellent restaurants. There's even a colonial-era tavern with Irish beer on tap, where Paul Revere was once a regular customer.

🚶 the walk

▶ **To begin the walk starting at the MBTA Green or Orange Line Stations, turn right onto Causeway Street, then left onto Washington Street. Cross the bridge and turn right.**

The *Charlestown Navy Yard (1),* established in 1800 and decommissioned in 1974, has many opportunities for exploration: the octagonal brick 1854 *Muster House;* the quarter-mile-long granite 1834 *Ropewalk* where rope was manufactured for the navy until 1960; the 1805 *Commandant's House;* the *1833 Drydock 1,* still in use; the USS *Cassin Young,* of the World War II South Pacific "tin can fleet"; the USS *Constitution,* aka *Old Ironsides,* built in 1797 and the oldest commissioned ship in the U.S. Navy. ▶ **Retrace Constitution**

Road toward the bridge. Turn right.

The site of Charlestown's municipal government from 1630 until annexation by Boston in 1874, *City Square (2)* languished until recently under both an elevated railway and an elevated highway. A subway replaced the El, while the Big Dig replaced the elevated highway with a tunnel and a new park on top, designed with community help. In the park's center are the preserved foundations of John Winthrop's 1639 Great House, torched during the Battle of Bunker Hill.
▶ **Follow Harvard Street away from the square.**

Town Hill (3) was partially cut down after the fire during the Battle of Bunker Hill. The local array of building styles follows the street plan that Thomas Graves prepared for John Winthrop in 1629. *Harvard Place* is paved with plate-shaped "hobblestones" set on end, believed to be original seventeenth-century paving. *John Harvard Mall* commemorates the church where Harvard preached until his death in 1638, when half his library was bequeathed to support his namesake university. Farther up Main Street the *1822 Austin Block* was built by General Nathaniel Austin from stone quarried at Outer Brewster Island in Boston Harbor.

Federal-period buildings near *Thompson Square (4)*, also on Main Street, survived mostly untouched until the 1970s because the El on Main Street discouraged new construction. The *1794 Thompson House,* built at 119 Main Street by Timothy Thompson, who fought at Bunker Hill, was also occupied by Timothy's son, a U.S. congressman, and by Gardener Colby, who endowed Colby College. The *1780 Warren Tavern* commemorates General Joseph Warren, fallen hero of Bunker Hill. Paul Revere convened his Masonic lodge here for twenty years. The *1795 Hurd House,* 65–71 Main Street, is Charlestown's best example of Georgian architecture. Deacon John Larkin, who lived at 55–61 Main Street, loaned his horse Brown Beauty to Paul Revere for his midnight ride. ▶ **Turn right onto Warren Street and continue to**

BOB BERGMAN, MARKETING IMAGES

USS *Constitution*, Charlestown Navy Yard.

the corner of Winthrop Street. Turn left.

St. Mary's Church (5) served Charlestown's growing Irish community. Religious structures served as magnets for Yankee unease as Irish immigration increased; St. Mary's was attacked by an angry mob in 1853. By the time the current church was built in 1887, Irish Catholics were the majority.

John Boyle O'Reilly, who personified the growing acceptance of Irish in Boston, lived nearby and was editor of the *Pilot*, the newspaper of Boston's Catholic archdiocese.

Military training dominated the *Training Field (Winthrop Square) (6)* from 1632 until the Civil War. The Training Field was part of the battlefield of Bunker Hill. The heroic statue in the middle honors Charlestown's Civil War soldiers and sailors. Surrounding the field is a colorful cluster of Federal-period clapboard houses, contrasting with larger, brick row houses. ▶ **Follow along the left of the field and climb the hill.**

The *Bunker Hill Monument (7)* marks the battle on Breed's Hill (the original plan was to defend from Bunker Hill, the next hill over), when colonial troops, fueled by a little bravado (and perhaps a bit of rum), moved toward British troops massed on the harbor. The monument was dedicated in 1843 with a stirring oration by Daniel Webster and a less memorable speech by President John Tyler.

Monument Square (8) reflects Charlestown's social history. The grand 1848 double bow-fronted house at 7 Monument Square was built for a Charlestown mayor; *The Bostonians* was in part filmed here. Two mansions converted to rooming houses were the subject the 1952 book *Rooms to Let* by Helen Rush, about World War II and the Navy Yard. The old Charlestown High School at 30 Monument Square drew racially tinged strife during busing for school desegregation, as documented in *Common Ground* by J. Anthony Lukas. ▶ **Follow High Street, on the west side of the square.**

Near Bunker Hill a workers' community took hold, transforming the Yankees' ancient Century Club, at 44 High Street, into the local home of the *Knights of Columbus (9)*. The Knights persuaded John Fitzgerald Kennedy, campaigning for his first congressional election, to undergo initiation by marching a goat through Charlestown streets. ▶ **Turn right on Sullivan Street.**

As the population of Charlestown increased to a peak of

forty-two thousand by 1900—three times what it is today—every square inch of available land was covered with housing. To improve access, *Forty Flights (10)* (seven flights of stairs) were built. ❱ **Turn left on Russell Street. Forty Flights starts on the right, opposite the end of Mead Street. To avoid the climb, follow Sullivan Street to Bunker Hill Street.**

The effort of climbing Forty Flights is rewarded by an expansive view from the *real Bunker Hill (11)*. The peaceful burial ground for Irish immigrants (closed to the public) in back of the 1859 *St. Francis de Sales Church* was established in 1830, over opposition and lawsuits by Charlestown's city government. Down below, *Doherty Playground* has sweeping views of the Mystic River. Follow the curving granite steps leading through the playground toward the riverbank. ❱ **Turn left on Medford Street and left again onto Baldwin Street. Turn right on Bunker Hill Street.**

Baldwin Street buildings are almost entirely brick, reminiscent of Beacon Hill. At 95 Baldwin Street, a charming clapboard house is only 12 feet wide. The *Charlestown Working Theatre,* a lively community playhouse at 442 Bunker Hill Street, was once a fire barn. Next to the theater, the award-winning *Charlestown Community Garden* welcomes visitors all day.

The *Mystic River Waterfront (12)* is dominated by the former Schrafft's candy factory, with its vintage hot pink neon sign and enormous illuminated clocks. ❱ **Turn right at the Schrafft's Factory driveway; follow blue Harborwalk signs to the Mystic River.** Behind Schrafft's are absorbing riverside views of natural gas tankers, vessels hauling mountains of scrap metal, and huge container ships. Charlestown's waterfront sparked intensive union organizing in 1872 and remains an area of strong pro-labor sentiment. ❱ **Retrace your steps to Bunker Hill Street and turn right. Take the MBTA Orange Line train inbound from Sullivan Square Station.**

Visible from the train, *Bunker Hill Community College (13)* was built on the site of Charlestown State Prison, where Italian anarchists Sacco and Vanzetti were executed in 1927, and where Malcolm Little discovered the Muslim religion in 1948 and became Malcolm X. In another of the layers of history typical of Charlestown, recreation fields cover former ponds and locks of the Middlesex Canal. Across Rutherford Avenue is the seventeenth-century Phipps Street Burying Ground, where early Puritan colonists are buried along with some of the African Americans who lived in Charlestown before 1800. The granite obelisk on top of the burial hill is an 1828 memorial to John Harvard.

▶ **The walk returns to North Station, completing a loop.**

KATHRYN AND RICHARD DOWNING *have lived in Charlestown for twenty-five years.*

 **walk 8**

Hyde Park and Victorian Fairmount

Start and finish: Hyde Park Avenue and River Street, Hyde Park

Getting there: Take the commuter rail from South Station/Back Bay Station to Hyde Park Station; or take a No. 32 bus from the Forest Hills MBTA Orange Line Station to Cleary Square

Getting back: Return on the Commuter Rail Line, or take the No. 32 bus to Forest Hills

Time: 1 hour

Distance: 2 miles

Difficulty: Moderate—some uphill grades

Accessibility: Fully wheelchair accessible

Rest rooms: Hyde Park Municipal Building, 1179 River Street; Hyde Park Library, 35 Harvard Avenue

ON A HILLSIDE overlooking the Neponset River lies a little Victorian time capsule amid more modern structures—that part of Hyde Park known as Fairmount. This walk will take you up and down Fairmount's steep streets on a trip back in time past stunning and fascinating structures.

Together with Cleary Square, Hyde Park's shopping and administrative center, Fairmount occupies Boston's southern-most tip; it's farther from downtown than any other part of

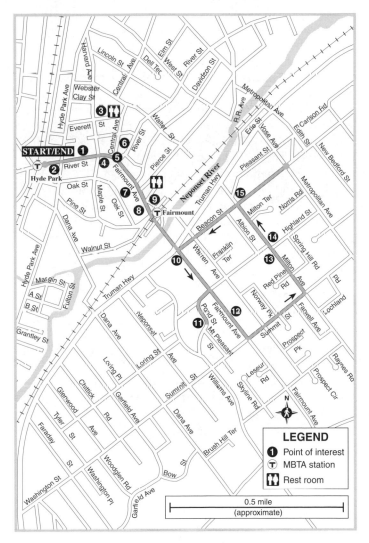

Hyde Park and Victorian Fairmount

the city. This remote location meant that Fairmount was somewhat of a late bloomer among Boston neighborhoods and is why it peaked in the Victorian period.

The pivotal event in Fairmount's development was the 1856 arrival of a group known as the Twenty Associates. These businessmen came to town soon after the railroads did and built twenty Italianate-style houses on Fairmount Avenue. The elegant homes sparked dramatic growth. Within short order, streetcar lines had been extended to Hyde Park, and an impressive number of fine residential, commercial, public, and church buildings had been erected.

Hyde Park remained an independent town until 1912, when its residents voted to join Boston. As this walk will reveal to you, the Fairmount neighborhood retains several of its original twenty homes and, with them, its own unique identity. It is an enclave of Victoriana on its hillside overlooking the Neponset.

🚶 the walk

Cleary Square (1) is distinguished by a large grouping of retail businesses concentrated along River Street and Fairmount Avenue. ▶ **Follow River Street east, away from the railroad overpass.** The *Cleary Square Post Office (2)* occupies the site of the first Kennedy's Department Store. During the 1920s, Kennedy's moved to Boston and joined the downtown group of large department stores.

Just a few steps off your route, the 1899 *Hyde Park Branch Library (3)* at 35 Harvard Avenue houses Weld Hall, named for noted abolitionist Theodore Weld. A designated National Register and Boston Landmark building, it retains its original 18-foot-high Georgian Revival reading room with Siena marble floors, oak fireplace, and fluted Corinthian pilasters. At 1220 River Street, the 1894 *Christ Episcopal Church (4)* was designed by architect Ralph Adams Cram in the modern

Gothic style. ❯ **Continue on River Street as it curves to the southeast.**

On the traffic island where River Street joins Fairmont Avenue, you'll find the *Hyde Park clock (5)*. At the clock's dedication in 1998, a time capsule was buried, to be excavated at Hyde Park's 200th anniversary in 2056. Just behind is the 1921 *Municipal Building (6)*, 1179 River Street, designed by Desmond and Lord in the neoclassical Georgian Revival style, serving as a community center with an auditorium, a gymnasium, meeting rooms, and offices. ❯ **Follow Fairmount away from the square.**

The *Everett Square Theatre (7)*, 9 Fairmount, built in 1875, has a mural on its facade. At first featuring vaudeville, it later became a movie house until its closure in 1984.

The *Riverside Theater Works (8)*, 49–51 Fairmount, offers training in the performing arts for children and adults—five former students appeared in Broadway shows in 2002. Built in 1897, it was originally named French's Opera House, for its developer.

At Fairmount and Nott Street stood Methodist Hall, the *site of the first women's vote (9)*. Here a group of courageous women voted in a local election in 1870, for the first time in U.S. history. They cast ballots in a box specially set out for them. ❯ **Cross carefully at Truman Highway and continue up the hill on Fairmount Avenue.**

The Gothic Revival *William Badger House (10)*, at 181 Fairmount Avenue, was built in 1857 for the man who was the stairbuilder for each of the first twenty houses built in Fairmount. ❯ **Turn right onto Highland Street and then veer left onto Pond Street for a brief detour.**

The *Charles Haley House (11)*, 9 Pond Street, was built between 1885 and 1888 in the Queen Anne style, with a wraparound porch and an original Queen Anne barn painted in Victorian colors. ❯ **Retrace your steps to Fairmount and turn right.**

Back on Fairmount Avenue is the site where the town's *original twenty homes (12)* were built. Their fashionable Italianate-style of construction in a bucolic suburb drew attention to Hyde Park. In 1864 one of these homes, formerly standing at 212 Fairmount Avenue, was sold to abolitionist Theodore Weld, whose wife, Angelina, and sister-in-law, Sarah Grimké, were suffragettes and abolitionists. Sarah made history as the first woman to address the state legislature; she was submitting a petition supporting both the abolition of slavery and women's suffrage, signed by twenty thousand people. The *George Washburn House,* 230 Fairmount Avenue, is a turreted 1894 Queen Anne residence built and occupied by a Boston merchant. Master builder George Pierce, who helped build "The Twenty," constructed the 1857 *Italianate residence* at 265 Fairmount Avenue. The *John Williams House*, 281 Fairmount Avenue, was built in 1856 as a residence for this early settler and master builder. It is the only Twenty Associates' house that retains its original clapboards. Of the original homes, this is the best preserved. ❱ **Turn left onto Summit Street and proceed to the corner of Milton Avenue. Turn left.**

Milton Avenue (13) is another hilly street parallel to Fairmount Avenue. It is, arguably, even more elegant. The *Horatio Kaynes House,* 79 Milton Avenue, in 1860s French mansard style, features its original clapboards and architectural details. The owner was a sea captain and Civil War blockade runner. A good example of a *mansard-style house* is the residence at 75 Milton Avenue, built between 1867 and 1871; it retains its original scalloped and slate roof and period barn. At the corner of Highland Street (96 Highland), the turreted Queen Anne *George E. Whiting House (14)* was built in 1888 for the president of the Hyde Park Electric Light Company. A little farther along on Milton Avenue is the site of the *Archibald Grimké House,* 60 Milton Avenue, built by the editor and publisher of the *Hub,* a newspaper pressing for equal rights. When he headed the local NAACP branch, it

A home in Hyde Park's Fairmount district.

became the country's largest. ❱ **Proceed to Beacon Street and turn right.**

Beacon Street (15) is lined with Victorian houses. The *Fred Tirrell House,* 60 Beacon Street, is an 1886 turreted Queen Anne built for a Boston boot merchant. The *James Tilden House,* a Colonial Revival residence at 66 Beacon Street, was built for the inventor whose water meters were used all over the world. Master builder John Williams built himself an *Italianate-style house* at 71 Beacon Street in 1869. Later the house was updated to its present elaborate Queen Anne style. Note the Gothic barn in the rear.

❱ **Follow Beacon Street to Fairmount Avenue. From here you can return to Cleary Square for access to public transportation lines.**

Prepared by members of WalkBoston.

 **walk 9**

Jamaica Plain

Start and finish: Intersection of Centre and South Streets, Jamaica Plain
Getting there: Take the MBTA No. 39 bus from Copley Square in Boston to the Monument Square stop
Getting back: Take the MBTA No. 39 bus on Centre Street to Copley Square
Time: 2 hours
Distance: 3 miles
Difficulty: Easy
Accessibility: Fully wheelchair accessible
Rest rooms: Jamaica Pond (seasonal)

AFFECTIONATELY KNOWN AS "J.P.," Jamaica Plain is one of the greenest neighborhoods in the city—surrounded on three sides by large tracts of forested and much-loved open space. With bucolic Arnold Arboretum, picturesque Jamaica Pond, expansive Franklin Park, and historic Forest Hills Cemetery, Jamaica Plain is an outdoor oasis.

Still, don't let all the natural beauty obscure J.P.'s abundance of architectural intrigue. The neighborhood hosts a number of spectacular "Painted Lady" Victorians on Sumner Hill. Stately mansions line Jamaica Pond and nearby streets.

These days J.P. hosts wealthy "hip" suburbanites returning to the city, plus a large Hispanic and Caribbean population.

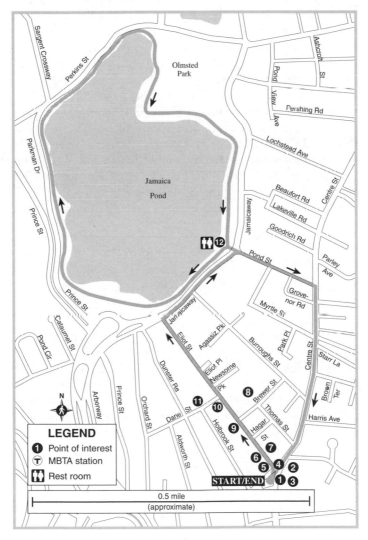

Jamaica Plain

They join longtime Irish Catholic residents, a lesbian/gay contingent, students, and many others. This walk gives you a sampling of what they perhaps love best about J.P.: quiet residential streets, spectacular mansions, a vibrant commercial district, and—most of all—Jamaica Pond, a major park and haven for the city-weary.

Oh, and incidentally . . . if you're like most visitors, you're wondering, "How did Jamaica Plain get its name?" Tradition holds that a Native American chief named Katchemakin inhabited these lands before European settlers arrived; over the years his name became corrupted to *Jamaica*. The *Plain* part may simply refer to the abundance of flat, arable land that was once used for farming and grape growing. Today it's used for recreation and rejuvenation, as you'll discover on this walk through Boston's green heart.

🚶 the walk

▶ **This walk opens at the intersection of Centre and South Streets.** *Monument (Eliot) Square (1),* here at the starting point, was the early center of the community. The Civil War Monument stands on what was once the town green, bordered by early clapboard structures. Built in 1871, the monument honors residents of the area who died in the Civil War while serving in one of the four branches of the armed services— infantry (crossed rifles), artillery (cannon), cavalry (sabers), and navy (anchor). Nearby, a much smaller stone monument commemorates fallen Revolutionary War soldiers.

Facing the monument is the *Loring-Greenough House (2),* a Georgian mansion built in 1760 and one of J.P.'s last surviving colonial residences in its original form. Joshua Loring, a retired British Royal Navy officer, built it before his family fled in the face of local patriot sentiment. Confiscated by colonial troops, it was used as one of the first military hospitals in the country. After being purchased by Anne Doane and David Greenough in 1784, five generations of the family lived here. In 1924 the Jamaica Plain Tuesday Club, a women's social club, purchased the building to preserve it as a museum.

To the right is *Curtis Hall (3)*, named for an early settler of Jamaica Plain. Once the town hall of West Roxbury (which encompassed Jamaica Plain), the structure now houses a community recreation center and swimming pool.

A *Stone Mile Marker (4)* sits just outside the fence at the Civil War Monument. Shaped like an oversized cemetery stone, this 5-mile marker was set in 1735 on the route between Boston and Providence to help eighteenth-century horse riders and walkers stay on course. The distance marked here is measured from the Old State House in downtown Boston. ❿ **Cross to the church and follow Eliot Street.**

The *First Church of Jamaica Plain (5)*, Jamaica Plain's oldest, was also known as the Third Church of Roxbury when J.P. was part of Roxbury. The early wooden church that stood here was replaced by the present granite English Gothic structure in 1853. The church houses a grand organ that is occasionally used to make recordings.

On the same side of the street is the *Ancient Burial Ground (6)*, J.P.'s oldest cemetery, established in 1785. Three of the local men who marched against the retreating British on April 19, 1775, are buried here. Revolutionary War captain Lemuel May and early members of former governor Weld's family lie in the burial ground. By the 1850s the cemetery was no longer active. It is sometimes possible to enter it by walking up to the church; the gate to the cemetery is on the right.

Across the street, the *Footlight Club (7)*, at 7 Eliot Street, is the oldest community theater in America—still alive and well and presenting high-quality amateur theatrical shows. Its home, Eliot Hall, was built in 1831 and once served as town hall and as a parish building for the First Church; it's found on the National Register of Historic Places. Joey McIntyre, a member of the erstwhile singing group New Kids on the Block, first performed on this stage. Later, when he hit the big time, he funded the 1990 renovation of the hall. ▶ **Continue down Eliot until you come to a large, fenced expanse of lawn surrounding a boxy structure on the left.**

The *Eliot School (8)* is an early building that retains much of its original facade and interior. Although the building dates to 1831, the school was founded in 1676. The school was progressive from the start, accepting students of every background—white, Indian, and black. Early teachers were paid in corn. Today it houses an institute of applied arts, with classes in upholstery, stained glass, sewing, and cabinetry.

The *Ellen Swallow Richards House (9)* at 32 Eliot Street was home to the first woman to enroll at the Massachusetts Institute of Technology (MIT) in 1871. A renowned scientist, she later taught sanitary engineering at her alma mater, emphasizing clean food and water and establishing home economics as a field of study. At the time she lived in this house, MIT was located in Copley Square, an easy commute. ▶ **Turn right onto Brewer Street. Go halfway down and stop in front of the peach-colored house on the left.**

An *architectural sampler (10)* of buildings, Brewer Street is virtually packed with architectural history. A gray house features a mansard roof, which creates an extra floor. The next house, a bright orange Victorian, features hallmarks of Queen Anne style: asymmetry, with divisions between courses of shingles. The C. S. Smith House, built in 1843 in Gothic Revival style, boasts a carved bargeboard beneath its eaves. All three homes have matching barns behind them. ▶ **Return to Eliot Street, turn right, and proceed to Dane Street.**

One of the last of the great mansions in the area, the *Dane Street Mansion (11)*, sits a few steps down on the right side of Dane Street. The enormous Greek Revival manse, with bold columns and an unusual cupola, has been home to the same family for more than a hundred years. ▶ **Return to Eliot**

Civil War monument, Monument Square, Jamaica Plain.

Street, turn left, and continue to street's end. Turn right onto Jamaicaway, crossing at the Pond Street crosswalk.

You are at *Jamaica Pond (12)*, a 70-acre body of water that in the nineteenth century provided ice and drinking water to the citizens of Boston. Here you can sit on a bench and enjoy the sparkling waters or views of summer boating. In winter, enter the Boathouse, where you may be able to warm yourself at the fireplace. Take the approximately 30-minute (1.5-mile) walk around the pond on a tree-lined path. This is a popular recreation spot. ▶ **After looping around Jamaica Pond, take Pond Street east to Centre Street to return to this walk's starting point.**

This segment of Centre Street features many good restaurants and independently owned shops. Take a stroll!

RHEA BECKER *is president of the Jamaica Plain Historical Society and a longtime professional journalist.*

 **walk 10**

Roslindale

Start and finish: Roslindale Square

Getting there: Take any bus from the MBTA Orange Line
  Forest Hills Station along Washington Street to
  Roslindale Square

Getting back: Any bus from Roslindale Square toward the
  MBTA Orange Line Forest Hills Station

Time: 3¹⁄₂ hours

Distance: 2.5 miles

Difficulty: Generally easy; steep hills to the Arboretum

Accessibility: Wheelchair accessible except for downhill route
  leaving Arboretum

Rest rooms: Roslindale Municipal Building; public library

THE FRAGRANCE of piping-hot breads and pastries fills the air
in Roslindale Square early every morning. Bakeries abound
here: at last count there were seven in and around the village.
They reflect the ethnic mix of the neighborhood, with delica-
cies rooted in Greek, Arab, Italian, Spanish, and American
cultures. Restaurants in the square serve foods from Japan,
Italy, China, and the Caribbean. Many have verandas for
alfresco dining.

Roslindale's numerous food options are the focus of the
down-to-earth and charming neighborhood you'll explore in
this walk. Around the vigorous commercial area of Roslindale

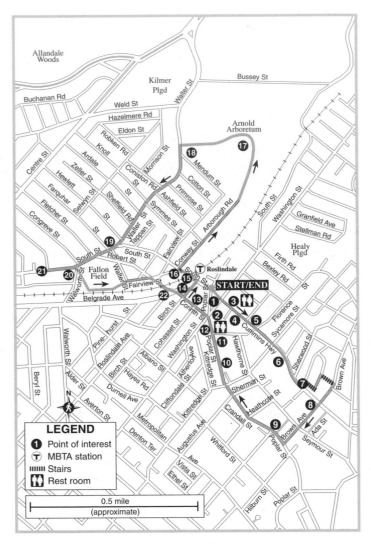

Roslindale Village

Square, Victorian residences line the hills and dales. Generous green spaces and narrow streets keep traffic from overwhelming the village. Topping one of the hills amid these quiet enclaves, you'll gain an astoundingly beautiful view of downtown Boston over a sea of green trees.

You'll also view a cornucopia of Roslindale's architectural highlights, which reflect a diversity of styles and influences fitting for this multiethnic community. Roslindale, as you'll see, is a center of Greek culture and activities—reflected today in churches and a monument to Alexander the Great—while numerous other ethnic communities now also call it home, attracted by its small-town ambience and relaxed lifestyle. The community is equally diverse in housing types, with "doctors' houses" mixing with less grand structures. Most retain a lived-in look. It is a comfortable place that invites strolling . . . and eating.

🚶 the walk

▶ **The walk begins and ends in the landscaped triangular open space at the center of Roslindale, where all bus lines converge.**

Roslindale Square (1) is the center of the community. Officially it is Irving Adams Square, named in honor of the first Massachusetts hero of World War I. The land was lined with stores until it was cleared for the memorial park in 1919. The park nearly became a major traffic rotary in the 1960s but was saved by Roslindale's vigilant citizens. ▶ **Proceed southeast down Cummins Highway.**

Public buildings are concentrated along the south side of the square, and the view from Cummins reveals a charming grouping. Before crossing Washington, you'll spot the *Roslindale Branch Library (2)* on the right, a low, domed building of the 1960s with curved exterior walls following the street line, and the *Roslindale Municipal Building (3),* a prominent local landmark (built in 1916) that provides a central location for state and city services. Across Cummins Highway is the Boston Elevated Railway power substation (1911). Behind it, but also part of the civic center, the Romanesque-style *Roslindale Congregational Church (4)* designed by Boston architect James Murray features projecting bays, dormers and entrance porticoes, and a high clock tower. Also look for the 1880s *Roslindale Baptist Church (5),* with shingles and exposed framing that combine identifiable details of the Stick-and Shingle-styles. ❿ **Continue along Cummins Highway.**

The Classical Revival *Washington Irving School (6)* (1936) is distinguished by three entrance bays, each with rounded arches, and a balustrade topping the wall at the horizontal parapet.

Farther down the highway, the *Johnswood Stairway (7)* offers a direct route for hill residents down an abrupt hill to Brown Avenue. If you like, you can bypass this hill by walking up Cummins to the next landmark on your tour, the *Sacred Heart Church (8).* This building's prominent tower can be seen from many parts of Roslindale. Catholics moving into the area used a tent for services until the yellow brick Victorian Gothic church was completed in 1895. The original brick tower was taken down in 1950 and replaced by a metal spire. Near the church parish house on Cummins Highway is a stone grotto lined with flowers, holding a replica of Michelangelo's famed *Pietà.* ❿ **From the church, turn right onto Brown Avenue, then right onto Poplar Street.**

The *oldest house in Roslindale (9),* hidden behind its neighbors at 266 Poplar Street, is a pre–Revolutionary War house dating to 1725. Originally a half Cape, the house was extended to the right of the entry in 1775. Windows in the earlier section were likely enlarged at that time. The house was renovated in both the nineteenth and twentieth centuries

FORNAX BAKERY

Fresh locally baked bread, Roslindale Square.

with new windows and sidelights around the main entrance.

Farther along Poplar you'll find the 1926 *Roslindale High School (10)*, abandoned as a school and renovated for residential units in the 1980s. Town records claim there is a stone panel with the city insignia at the cornice line. Running alongside the high school, *Florence Street (11)* features a row of Colonial Revival houses built around the early 1900s and painted in bright colors, reflecting eclectic designs with some Craftsman-style elements.

As you proceed down Poplar to Washington Street, note the 1928 *Parkway Building (12)* at the corner. Art deco elements include vertical spandrels that are capped with ziggurat embattlements. It houses—what else?—a bakery! ❯ **Beyond Washington Street, veer left onto Corinth Street (13), the business center of Roslindale.**

Corinth was laid out in the 1880s as a link between Washington Street and the railroad station. ❯ **Turn right onto Birch Street (14).** This area has recently been taken over by small boutiques. ❯ **At South Street, turn left.**

The *Roslindale Commuter Rail Station (15)* is constructed with a narrow pedestrian underpass that is a shortcut for walkers to connect two portions of South Street. The *School of Modern Languages (16),* the former Church of Our Savior, resembles a fifteenth-century English country church with modern Gothic touches. ❯ **Turn right onto Conway Street, which soon becomes Arborough Road.**

Peter's Hill at the Arnold Arboretum (17) offers one of the best views in Boston anywhere. The arboretum—part of Harvard University—specializes in preserving specimens of all types of vegetation; among other examples, it now holds 130 different kinds of maple trees! Its 265 acres of landscaped hills and walkways form a major boundary for Roslindale and an essential and welcome open space for the community.

Bussey Bridge, at the bottom of the hill, was the sight of a much-publicized 1887 tragedy: the weight of a commuter train caused the bridge to collapse onto South Street. The media headlined the event, and sightseers thronged to see the broken bridge and shattered train cars. Ironically, the disaster may have attracted new residents to Roslindale, when gawkers took in the beauty of the area. ❯ **Follow a dirt path down the hill.**

Look for the *site of the first meetinghouse (18)* in Roslindale, built in 1711; only the old burying ground remains at the site. ◗ **At Walter Street, turn left, then fork right onto South Street.** At the corner of South Street the *Longfellow School (19),* built in 1897, was renovated for residences in the 1990s. The massive structure bears elements of a manor house, with Renaissance and Classical Revival features at entries and windows, and steep pitched roofs with pointed dormers.

Just beyond the park along South Street is *Doctors' Row (20)*—a row of Colonial Revival and Craftsman-style homes built between 1895 and 1906. Across the street look for the *Russian Orthodox Church of the Epiphany (21),* an onion-dome church built in 1975. ◗ **Walk through Fallon Field to Fairview Street, and turn right under the railroad bridge to Corinth Street.**

The return trip to Roslindale Village passes the glistening white *Alexander the Great Memorial (22),* a bust of the ancient conqueror on a pedestal. A gift to Boston from Athens, Greece, the monument stands in a small park that was once a gas station.

◗ **The walk ends back at Roslindale Village.** You are advised to visit one of the many bakeries for a special treat!

CATHY SLADE *is president of the Roslindale Historical Society.*

 **walk 11**

Savin Hill

Start: Savin Hill MBTA Red Line Station
Getting there: Take the MBTA Red Line, Ashmont Branch, to Savin Hill
Finish: Savin Hill or UMass/Columbia Point MBTA Red Line Station
Getting back: Take the MBTA Red Line
Time: 1 hour
Distance: 2 miles, or extend to 4.3 miles
Difficulty: Moderate climbs via streets and stairways on hills
Accessibility: Savin Hill Station and Savin Hill Park are not fully wheelchair accessible
Rest rooms: Bathhouse at Malibu Beach (seasonal)

SAVIN HILL, a very distinctive part of Boston, sits serenely above a tangle of teeming transportation arteries. Its elevation isolates it from the rest of the city, protecting it from the heavy traffic on the expressways, railroads, and highways at its feet. Because there are usually few cars on its streets, Savin Hill can be easily and safely explored on foot. And indeed the neighborhood has much to offer the walker, including a delightful jumble of residential architectural styles lining streets that circle the hill to the park at its very top. Here you can enjoy views of the sea, downtown Boston, and the peninsula housing the University of Massachusetts Boston and the

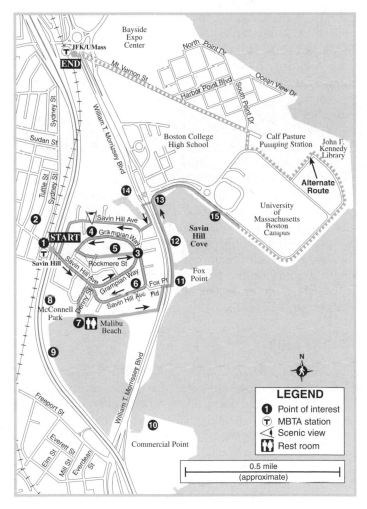

Bayside
Expo
Center

North Point Dr

JFK/UMass

END

Mt. Vernon St

Harbor Point Blvd

South Point Dr

Ocean View Dr

Sydney St

Sudan St

Boston College
High School

Calf Pasture
Pumping Station

John F.
Kennedy
Library

Alternate
Route

Tuttle St

Sydney St

②

① **START**

Savin Hill

④ Savin Hill Ave

Grampian Way

⑭

⑬

⑮

Savin
Hill
Cove

University
of
Massachusetts
Boston
Campus

Savin Hill Ave

⑤

③

Rockmere St

⑫

Denny St

Grampian Way

⑥

Fox Pl

⑪

Fox
Point

Savin Hill Ave Rd

⑧

McConnell
Park

⑦ 🚻 Malibu
Beach

⑨

N

William T. Morrissey Blvd

William T. Morrissey Blvd

Freeport St

Everett St

⑩

Commercial Point

Elm St

Mill St

Everdean St

LEGEND

① Point of interest

Ⓣ MBTA station

◁ Scenic view

🚻 Rest room

0.5 mile
(approximate)

Savin Hill

John F. Kennedy Library—as well as Savin Hill's own ocean beach and two yacht clubs.

The neighborhood dates to 1630, when (before settling Boston) Puritans landed from the ship *Mary and John* and built a temporary settlement for about 140 people on what they called Rock Hill. By the 1800s the arrival of transportation—railroad, subway, and eventually highways—transformed Savin Hill. These new arteries first connected the area to Boston; it became one of the city's first suburbs. Yet ironically, they also isolated it.

When it was cut off from the ocean by Morrissey Boulevard in the early 1930s, Savin Hill became an increasingly identifiable neighborhood. Its separation was compounded by the wide trench of the Southeast Expressway in the late 1950s. Still, being cut off from, the outside world has enhanced, rather than detracted from its neighborly feeling and livability. Described in an old history of the Savin Hill Yacht Club as a "delightful semi-marine paradise of peaceful luxury, with yachts and horses," the neighborhood has dropped some of the luxury, yachts, and horses but has remained delightful. For many of its residents—and visiting walkers—it is a paradise.

🚶 the walk

The *Savin Hill MBTA Station (1)* was once a station on the Old Colony Railroad between Boston and Plymouth. The new railroad spurred development when it opened in 1845. It also created the first major barrier between the Savin Hill community and the rest of Boston. ▶ **Begin your walk heading northwest down Savin Hill Avenue.**

Down the street from the MBTA station is the *Savin Hill Mural (2),* unveiled in November 1999. The mural was created by Savin Hill residents, assisted by teenagers from the Colonel Daniel Marr Boys and Girls Club. It depicts the daily life of Native American residents in Savin Hill five hundred years ago. Across Tuttle Street, St. Williams School is on the site of an early luxury hotel whose owner dubbed the area Savin Hill in 1819 to provide what he thought to be a more elegant name for the area. ▶ **Retrace your steps and cross the bridge over the Southeast Expressway on Savin Hill Avenue. Veer left onto Grampian Way.**

Grampian Way forms almost a complete loop around the base of Savin Hill and hosts some of the oldest homes on the hill. The lower portion of *Savin Hill Park (3)* is a favorite sledding slope for local children with a monument commemorating the brief 1630 landing of the Puritans here before they moved across the harbor to Boston. The settlers' landing is commemorated annually with a celebration in June in conjunction with Dorchester Day ceremonies. After September 11, 2001, the stone commemorating the events of 1630 is decorated as an informal neighborhood memorial to the victims of the terrorist attacks. ▶ **Continue on Grampian Way as it circles and gradually climbs Savin Hill.**

Along the way, note the dramatic view from a *downtown skyline overlook (4)*. Here the hill is so steep that buildings are difficult to construct. Nevertheless, it is said that barracks were built on the north side of the hill along Grampian Way during the Revolutionary War.

At the top of the hill, stone steps lead to *Savin Hill Woods and Summit (5)* with a commanding view of Dorchester Bay, Quincy, and the Harbor Islands. Outcroppings of Roxbury puddingstone accentuate the landscape of this height-of-land 110 feet above the harbor. The best outlook is in fall or spring when fewer leaves obscure the 360-degree view.

You can descend the hill on steps leading to the *outer loop of Savin Hill Avenue (6)*. Grand Victorian seaside homes were built here around the beginning of the twentieth century to take advantage of the harbor, beach, and water views.

Malibu Beach (7) lies in a cove between Morrissey

Boulevard and the Southeast Expressway. Originally a natural gravel beach faced the ocean, but the cove was separated from the harbor by the creation of Morrissey Boulevard, and the beach became a park. The playground and ball fields of adjacent *McConnell Playground (8)* host many neighborhood activities. Just offshore, with a land connection at the park's edge, the *Dorchester Yacht Club (9)* is home to what was once the "Harrison Square crowd," racing rivals to the Savin Hill Yacht Club. ▶ **Walk east along the beach to Morrissey Boulevard**.

Look right for the *gas tank on Commercial Point (10)* on the far side of the boulevard. Keyspan (formerly Boston Gas) maintains this gas tank with its 1971 painting by Sister Corita Kent, intriguing for what appears to be a profile of Ho Chi Minh in blue looking toward downtown Boston. Commercial Point served as home to a number of whaling businesses in the 1830s and 1840s, along with the mansions of China trade merchants; these were cleared in 1888 to make room for the gas facility. ▶ **Look for the signalized pedestrian crossing on Morrissey Boulevard.**

Just ahead is the *Savin Hill Yacht Club (11),* which can trace its roots to 1875. The narrow navigation channel and the batterings of three disastrous hurricanes "failed to quench the spirit of the membership." ▶ **Cross Morrissey Boulevard and turn left.**

After a short distance you will see the *Dorchester Vietnam Veterans' Memorial (12)* on the right. Built in the 1990s after a long site-selection process, the memorial is carefully maintained by Dorchester's veterans, who host Memorial Day activities here every year.

The sidewalk becomes the *Harborwalk (13)* at the water's edge, leading around the peninsula of Columbia Point. In colonial times this area was known as the Calf Pasture. The marshes were filled over many years for utilities, housing, a prisoner-of-war barracks, and finally the present-day facilities. UMass Boston opened here in 1974, and the Kennedy Library in 1979. The Calf Pasture Pumping Station went out of use in 1968 when wastewater was rerouted to a new plant at Deer Island; it's now on the National Register of Historic Places. The view from the beginning of the Harborwalk includes UMass Boston and the Boston Harbor Islands.

Across the boulevard is *Patten's Cove (14)*, cut off when Morrissey Boulevard was built but once used by neighborhood residents for swimming and sailing. Nearby street names—Seaview Terrace, Wave Avenue—offer reminders that the area was once oceanfront. Horseshoe crabs can still be seen on the shores in mid-May. On the far side of the cove is the *Boston Globe* headquarters, located on an area that was landfilled in 1958.

As you walk southeast toward UMass Boston, look for *Fox Point Landing (15)*, a pier for UMass Boston marine research vessels near the mouth of the Neponset Estuary. It is also used to host the UMass Boston sailing program.

▶ **At this point you have two options. You can retrace your steps to the Savin Hill Red Line Station to conclude a 2-mile stroll. Or you can extend your walk in a loop around the Columbia Point peninsula. Continue past UMass Boston, the state archives building, the John F. Kennedy Library, and the Bayside Exposition Center to finish at the JFK/UMass Station on the MBTA Red Line—a total of 4.3 miles.**

ROSS HOWARD, *a senior at Boston Latin School, has lived in Savin Hill all his life. His parents,* JANE *and* ALFRED HOWARD, *are transportation consultants.*

South End

Start: Back Bay Station, MBTA Orange Line
Getting there: Take the MBTA Orange Line or commuter rail lines to MBTA Back Bay Station
Finish: Mass Avenue Station, MBTA Orange Line
Getting back: Take the MBTA Orange Line
Time: 1 hour
Distance: 2 miles
Difficulty: Easy
Accessibility: Fully wheelchair accessible
Rest rooms: Back Bay Station; Tent City; South End Public Library

WITH ITS PICTURESQUE architecture and wonderful mix of tolerant people, the South End is uniquely Boston. More than most neighborhoods, it is a community created by its residents to reflect their wide range of economic means, levels of social activism, and ethnic and racial backgrounds. This walk through the heart of the South End will give you a sampling of its vibrant streets and culture.

Much of what you'll see was designed in the mid-nineteenth century to attract Boston's wealthy merchant class. Home to the largest concentration of Victorian brick row houses in the country, the South End also contains grand homes, elegant parks, and mid-Victorian bow-front architec-

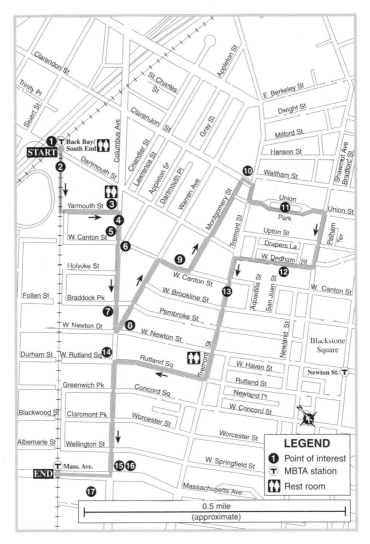

South End

Legend:
- ❶ Point of interest
- Ⓣ MBTA station
- 🚻 Rest room

0.5 mile
(approximate)

ture reminiscent of England. Look for bay windows, brownstone stoops, scrolled cast-iron railings, grand staircases, and ornate details.

The wealthy came . . . and then they moved on, largely to the Back Bay. By the turn of the twentieth century the South End was becoming a working-class, multicultural neighborhood. Immigrants from Ireland, Eastern Europe, Syria, Lebanon, China, and the West Indies joined African Americans moving from Beacon Hill or migrating from the South. To accommodate them most of the neighborhood homes were converted into lodging houses.

The newcomers made their mark: over the past hundred years South End residents have repeatedly organized to meet neighborhood needs. Initially settlement houses were established to serve low-income residents. Later, highway construction, urban renewal, and the civil rights struggle sparked residents to organize for local improvements.

When the South End was designated the nation's largest urban renewal area in the 1960s, residents came together again to protest housing demolition and to lobby for affordable housing. Empty lots became community gardens and parks. Street trees were planted. State plans for new highways were defeated. Residents designed, and the city adopted, a comprehensive "traffic-calming" plan to discourage through-traffic.

The twenty-first century has seen the South End's population shift one more time, its handsome old buildings attracting many professionals here to the shadows of Back Bay skyscrapers. Yet the more things change, the more they remain the same: the neighborhood continues to be known for both its diversity and its activism. This walk will take you through the community that residents have worked so hard to create. As you stroll along, appreciate the beauty of the big boulevards, sample some of Boston's best restaurants and jazz clubs, and be sure to wander down side streets. This is a great place to live and—of course—a great place to walk.

🚶 the walk

The *A. Philip Randolph statue (1)* in the Amtrak/Commuter Rail Line waiting area of Back Bay Station marks the start of this walk. Known as the Grandfather of the Civil Rights Movement, Randolph worked to desegregate labor unions, the armed forces, and the defense industry. He created the first black labor union, the Brotherhood of Sleeping Car Porters, in 1925. He was a lead organizer for the 1963 March on Washington, where he introduced Martin Luther King Jr. The statue, by sculptor Tina Allen, was part of MBTA's Arts on the Line program. **▶ Head southwest along the Southwest Corridor Park (2), crossing Dartmouth Street carefully.**

The corridor park stretches through the South End above the MBTA Orange Line and Amtrak. In 1972 community opposition defeated long-standing plans to build an expressway in this corridor. Making new use of highway funds, the transit line and park opened in 1987. **▶ Walk through the park, turning left onto Yarmouth Street.** As you turn the corner, notice an Orange Line vent stack cleverly deisgned to resemble a home.

Tent City (3), on the left, is named for the tent community pitched by some one hundred local residents in 1968 to dramatize the need for affordable housing on this site cleared for urban renewal. Twenty-two activists were arrested in the protest. Today Tent City serves as a model for mixed-income affordable housing, with 269 units and more than 800 residents. **▶ Turn right.**

Columbus Avenue (4) was built in 1868 and originally paved in wooden blocks to muffle the noise of carriages. In the style of French boulevards, it was aligned with the steeple of the Park Street Church to the left. Until the financial panic of 1873, Columbus Avenue and its elegant homes drew wealthy families to the neighborhood.

Methunion Manor (5), on the right facing Columbus

Avenue, was built in 1971. After serious financial problems, tenants organized to purchase the four buildings from the federal government. Today 151 families of low to moderate income live in these cooperatives. ◗ **Cross Columbus Avenue at West Canton Street.**

Allan Crite Square (6) honors an artist renowned for drawings, paintings, and prints that chronicle black community life in the South End and Roxbury. On this corner the 1976 traffic-calming plan is clearly visible. Two roadway lanes were removed to create the wide sidewalks on Columbus Avenue, and the square replaced vast areas of asphalt. Curbs were extended to provide pedestrian visibility for safer crossing and to slow turns onto Appleton Street. ◗ **Continue down Columbus Avenue.**

Across the street is *Charlie's Sandwich Shoppe (7),* a South End institution established in 1927 by a Greek immigrant named Charlie Poulis. It offered good, cheap meals twenty-four hours a day for the many boarders who lived in the South End in the 1950s. Famous jazz musicians such as Duke Ellington, Ray Charles, Sammy Davis Jr., and Johnny Hodges ate here after performing in segregated downtown clubs. Early meetings of the first black union, the Brother-hood of the Sleeping Car Porters, were held in secret on the second floor in the 1920s.

Diagonally across from Charlie's is *Harriet Tubman Memorial Park (8),* dedicated in honor of the ex-slave who led more than three hundred slaves to freedom on the Underground Railroad. ◗ **Turn left onto Warren Avenue.**

Hayes Park (9) lies to the right at West Canton Street on the site of a Boston church lost to arson. It includes a statue designed by Lebanese American sculptor Kahlil Gibran, *West Canton Street Child,* and two very old willows. ◗ **Turn right onto West Canton Street, then left onto Montgomery Street.** A gate between 74 and 78 Montgomery leads to a lovely private park.

MY TOWN

A. Philip Randolph statue, Back Bay Station.

At Clarendon Street is the *Boston Center for the Arts (10)*, formed in the 1960s for arts training and exhibitions, performances, and community gatherings. Facing Tremont Street is the Cyclorama, built in 1884 to house *The Battle of Gettysburg*—a large circular painting by Paul Philippoteau. ▶ **Turn right onto Tremont Street then left to head through Union Park.**

Designed in the 1850s, *Union Park (11)* epitomizes original South End elegance. Two fountains, an ornate fence, rococo ironwork, and a row of elm trees and flowers enhance the long, narrow park. At 20 Union Park is the former site of the South End House, Boston's first settlement house. ▶ **Turn right onto Shawmut Avenue and right again onto West Dedham Street.**

Villa Victoria (12) is a national model for community development by residents. In 1966 Puerto Rican tenants protesting demolition won the right to develop the site with 895 affordable housing units. In the plaza near the high-rise tower, a colorful tile mural honors Dr. Ramon Emeterio Betances, a nineteenth-century fighter for Puerto Rico's independence. ▶ **At Tremont Street (13), turn left.**

Community residents prevented this street from being widened as projected in 1960s state highway plans. Instead, it was narrowed and its sidewalks widened, encouraging many businesses to locate along the street. Look for the tall cupola of the Piano Craft Factory down the street, about ten blocks away. The South End's factories and warehouses provided work for immigrants at the turn of the twentieth century. ▶ **Turn right at the South End Library through lovely Rutland Square.**

Back on Columbus Avenue, note the soaring *Union United Methodist Church (14),* constructed in 1872 from Roxbury puddingstone. ▶ **Turn left down Columbus Avenue.**

The lion in front of 511 Columbus has been ridden by many children over the years. At 566 Columbus, in a modern building, the *United South End Settlements (15)* carries on the legacy of five settlement houses merged in 1959. The Hi-Hat, a nationally renowned nightclub, once stood here.

Just around the corner to the left, at 464 Massachusetts Avenue, the *Women's Service Club of Boston (16)* began as "Mrs. Wilson's Knitting Class" during World War I. Mary Evans Wilson and her friends knitted scarves and gloves for local black soldiers. In the late 1960s the club succeeded in making Massachusetts the first state to recognize domestic workers under state labor laws. ❱ **Turn right onto Massachusetts Avenue.**

In 1947 Joseph Lloyd Walcott became the first African American to open a nightclub in New England. *Wally's Café (17),* at 427 Massachusetts Avenue, welcomed Billie Holiday, Sarah Vaughn, and Charlie Parker, among others. Black performers and musicians stayed in local rooming houses because they were not allowed in downtown hotels. Local student musicians still play jazz here regularly. South End clubs were among the few places in Boston where races mixed comfortably.

Farther down the street Dr. Martin Luther King Jr. lived at 397 Massachusetts Avenue in 1952 and 1953 while completing his Ph.D. in philosophy at Boston University. While living here Dr. King led a march of more than twenty-two thousand people from the South End to Boston Common to protest school segregation and inadequate housing.

❱ **Continue on Massachusetts Avenue to the Southwest Corridor Park and end your walk at the Massachusetts Avenue Orange Line Station.**

KIM ALLEYNE *is the manager of Information and Research Practice at MYTOWN (Multicultural Youth Tour of What's Now).*

Part III

Exploring Neighborhoods Outside Boston

 **walk 13**

Arlington

Start: Alewife Station, MBTA Red Line or Arlington Center

Getting there: Take the MBTA Red Line to Alewife Station or take the No. 77 bus from Harvard Square Red Line Station to Arlington Center

Finish: Alewife or Harvard Square Stations, MBTA Red Line

Getting back: Walk to the MBTA Red Line Alewife Station or take the No. 77 bus from Arlington Center to the Red Line at Harvard Square Station

Time: 4 hours

Distance: 5 miles to Alewife Station

Difficulty: Easy to moderate

Accessibility: Fully wheelchair accessible

Rest rooms: Public library; town hall

AT FIRST GLANCE Arlington seems to be one more pleasant suburb of Boston—a good place to live without much for visitors to see. Not so. The town played a pivotal role in the American Revolution, as this stroll down the popular new Minuteman Rail-Trail and through the heart of town will reveal to you. Along the way you'll also discover its appealing restaurants, retail shops, and pond-studded green space.

Arlington was founded in the 1630s as a farming community, with mills to grind grain and process other types of

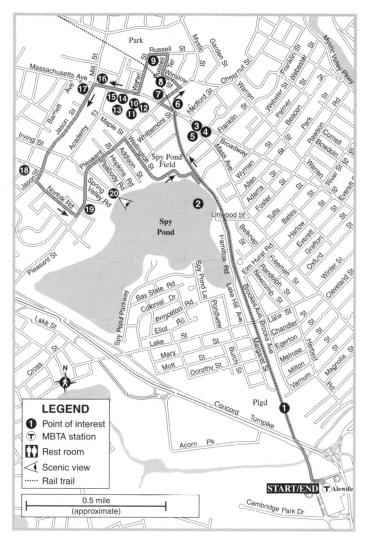

LEGEND

1 Point of interest
T MBTA station
Rest room
Scenic view
Rail trail

0.5 mile
(approximate)

Arlington

produce. It was first known as Menotomy—the Native American name for the area. It stepped into American history, however, on April 19, 1775.

On that date the townsfolk watched the main British force pass on their route to Concord. When lightly protected supply trains followed, Arlingtonians attacked. Their reward was the first British prisoners and stores captured in the Revolution.

Later that afternoon, as the redcoats were returning from Lexington and Concord, more desperate fighting took place here. Assuming that the British would return in a massed column, some seventeen hundred Minutemen from thirteen towns lined the stone walls on both sides of the old dirt road leading back to Boston. They fought with no coordination among units and with little information about the location of the redcoats. The British put out flanking parties that sandwiched the Minutemen between troops on the main road and troops in the fields. Pinned down, the Minutemen inflicted heavy casualties on the British and took heavy losses. Of the total redcoat casualties on that historic day, more than half took place in Menotomy. Likewise, more than half of the Americans who died that day perished along this portion of the historic battle road.

During the events of April 19, the British burned many buildings to flush out possible snipers. Yet several dating from the Revolutionary War period remain—surrounded now by an active, lively urban community and a cornucopia of architectural landmarks. Take a walk through Arlington—past and present.

🚶 the walk

▶ **The walk starts at the Alewife Station on the MBTA Red Line. Exit toward the parking garage. At the large, fish-shaped wooden benches, turn right to the street; cross carefully.**

You are at the start of the *Minuteman Rail-Trail (1),* a 10.5-mile asphalt path used for bicycling, walking, jogging, and in-line skating. Dedicated in 1992 as the country's 500th rail-trail, it roughly parallels Paul Revere's famous route through colonial Arlington and Lexington to warn colonists that "the British are coming!"

After a 15-minute walk along the rail-trail, look for *Spy Pond (2)*—a glacial remnant—on the left. The Reverend Cotton Mather once came here to fish and, like many other amateur fishermen, fell into the pond—"the boat being ticklish." Frightened British soldiers, pursued by Minutemen on April 19, 1775, jumped from supply train wagons and ran to the pond, where they threw their guns into the water, trying to keep the weapons from falling into the hands of the rebellious Minutemen. In the nineteenth century the pond became known for its ice; each winter some 250 men harvested up to 60,000 tons for shipment all over the world. The industry continued until 1930. ▶ **Leave the rail-trail at Swan Place. Turn right to head toward Massachusetts Avenue and the main business area of Arlington.**

Two blocks to your right is the octagonal *Central Fire Station (3),* a neo-Georgian building constructed in 1926. Behind lies the *Wayside Inn (4),* 393 Massachusetts Avenue, built before 1750 and now in the Broadway Historic District.

Across Massachusetts Avenue is the *Avon Place Historic District (5),* a small enclave of late-nineteenth-century buildings. At the main downtown intersection of Mystic Street and Massachusetts Avenue is the *Jefferson Cutter or Whittemore House (6),* 1 Whittemore Place, built before 1729. Inside the building is the Cyrus Dallin Art Museum, celebrating a local sculptor who became internationally famous. ▶ **Cross Mystic Street.**

In a small triangular park is the *Uncle Sam Monument (7).* Samuel Wilson, born in Arlington in 1766, founded a large meatpacking business and became inspector of provisions for soldiers from New York during the War of 1812. The federal monogram US was stamped on casks of beef and pork that were recognized as his products. The legend grew among soldiers that the letters stood for "Uncle Sam Wilson." The story survived, and Uncle Sam was later adopted for army recruiting campaigns.

Behind the Uncle Sam Monument and along the rail-trail is *Mill Brook (8),* which powered seven different Arlington mills for almost 250 years. The last one operating is the Old Schwamb Mill, turning out picture frames at a location farther out Massachusetts Avenue. For a tour, call (781) 643-0554. ▶ **Walk northeast down Mystic Street, turning left at Winslow Street.**

The *Russell Street Historic District (9)* has examples of the modest homes occupied by workers in nearby mills. ▶ **Take Russell Terrace, Russell Street, and Water Street to return to Massachusetts Avenue. Turn right.**

Along the left side of Massachusetts Avenue is a marvelous civic center comprised of public buildings and gardens. Many of these facilities honor the Robbins family, whose members were for generations among the leading citizens of Arlington. Their fortune was built on farming and distributing produce and meat in Boston. Look for the following landmarks:

- The 1892 Italian Renaissance–style *Robbins Library (10)* is found at 700 Massachusetts Avenue. The grand vaulted ceiling of the interior reading hall, glistening with hints of gold, is a civic monument.
- Behind the library is the *Whittemore-Robbins House (11),* the most imposing house in Arlington when it was built in c. 1800.
- Adjacent lies the *Old Burying Ground (12),* first used in 1730; in 1775 both Minutemen and British soldiers were buried here. In front of the cemetery stands the Unitarian First Parish Meetinghouse.

The Menotomy Indian Hunter by Cyrus Dallin, Arlington.

- The *Winfield Robbins Memorial Garden (13)* was established in 1913. At its center is Dallin's 1911 *Menotomy Indian Hunter.*
- The imposing 1913 *Robbins Memorial Town Hall (14)*, 730 Massachusetts Avenue, features an ornate open cupola surmounted by a pineapple, the traditional symbol of hospitality. Inside is a large meeting hall paneled in chestnut, with an elaborate carved and gilded coffered ceiling.
- Just beyond the town hall is the 1913 *Robbins Memorial Flagstaff (15)*, also sculpted by Cyrus Dallin.

▶ **Proceed west on Massachusetts Avenue.**

Beyond the civic buildings, on the right side of the avenue, is the notable Victorian-era *Greek Orthodox Church (16)*, named for St. Athanasius the Great. Some say it is the finest architectural monument in town. ▶ **Turn left onto Jason Street.**

At the corner is the *Jason Russell House (17)*, a colonial

building that dates to around 1740, with later additions. On April 19, 1775, it was the site of bloody fighting and of the deaths of Jason Russell and eleven Minutemen. Attached to the house is the charming Smith Museum, showcasing the history of Arlington. Both the house and museum are operated by the Arlington Historical Society, and are open April through October. ❯ **Follow Jason Street up the hill.**

Near the top of the hill is *Menotomy Rocks Park (18),* with its pond—the largest town recreation area. ❯ **When you leave the park, retrace your steps along Jason Street to Norfolk Road. Turn right onto Norfolk, go down the hill, and turn left (northeast) at Pleasant Street.** Here you can take a brief tour of the *Pleasant Street Historic District (19).* Homes along Spy Pond and the streets leading from it have been protected for their diversity and architectural interest.

Leave Pleasant Street for a brief detour down *Spring Valley Road (20).* At the foot of the street is a view over Spy Pond toward the downtown Boston skyline. At this location in 1810 the townsfolk constructed a powder house, designed to allow any potential explosion to spend itself harmlessly over the pond. The location was taken over in 1870 by the Arlington Boat Club, a popular social and athletic center. ❯ **Return to Pleasant Street, turn right, and proceed to Wellington Street, which leads to the banks of Spy Pond. Follow the pondside walkway to Pond Lane and return to the Minuteman Rail-Trail at Linwood Street.**

From here, you have several choices for the return walk: you can return to the Alewife Red Line Station via the Minuteman Rail-Trail or the No. 77 bus will return you from Arlington Center to MBTA's Harvard Square Red Line Station.

KATHY BAGDONAS and JIM EGAN *are members of WalkBoston.*

 **walk 14**

Chelsea

Start and finish: Bellingham Square, at the intersection of
   Fifth and Broadway in Chelsea
Getting there: Take the MBTA No. 111 Woodlawn–
   Haymarket bus from the MBTA's Haymarket Station,
   served by both the Green and Orange Lines
Getting back: Take the MBTA No. 111 Woodlawn–
   Haymarket bus to Haymarket Station, Boston
Time: 2½ hours
Distance: 3.5 miles
Difficulty: Moderate: some steps and gradual hills
Accessibility: Partially wheelchair accessible; two stairways
   that can be bypassed
Rest rooms: Police station; public library

AN UNEXPECTED DELIGHT, Chelsea offers a glorious setting,
restored downtown, civic center, and hilly views of the harbor
and downtown skyline. Looming over the city is the Tobin
Bridge—a dramatic landmark that is stunning seen from
below. The bridge and harbor setting highlight Chelsea's traditional role as a gateway into Boston.

Chelsea fronts on Boston Harbor, at the merging of two
rivers—the Mystic River from the west and the wide
Chelsea Creek from the northeast. This location has made it
a natural way station for products and people traveling into

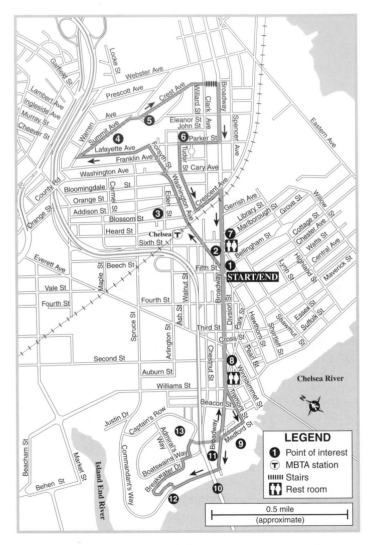

Chelsea

Boston from the moment its first European settlers arrived in 1624. Ferry service was initiated in 1631 and operated (albeit erratically) for centuries. As the metropolitan area grew, Chelsea became a welcome haven for immigrants to Massachusetts, providing inexpensive housing, ample job opportunities, and supportive social services. With the 1950 opening of the Tobin Bridge, Chelsea became an even more attractive location for living and for industry. Today the city is heavily influenced by its immigrants, for whom it remains an important stop on the path toward integration into American life.

This walk covers Chelsea end to end, ranging from Admiral Hill to Powderhorn Hill, both now capped by ancient military hospitals. Along the way you will see a dynamic city, always open to immigrant diversity. Look for the influence of ethnic traditions on the street life, restaurants, and shops in this small gateway to Boston.

the walk

Bellingham Square (1), where this walk begins, is the busy center of Chelsea, with its principal public buildings and shopping area and a Civil War monument in the center. *City Hall (2)* replaces buildings lost in the fire of 1908. This fire began in the Rag District, home of rag and waste salvagers forced out of Boston by new fire codes legislated in the wake of the Great Fire of 1872. The Rag District fire, spread by a high wind that blew burning rags high above the district, resulted in 492 acres burned to the ground along 18 miles of street, with three thousand buildings lost and eighteen thousand residents left homeless. Postdisaster, the state appointed a board of control to rebuild the city. Within twenty-nine months Chelsea had a new City Hall, new library, new hospital, two new firehouses, and 860 new buildings. The centerpiece was City Hall, designed by the Boston architectural firm of Peabody and Stearns. ❱ **Follow Washington Avenue over the active commuter rail station.**

On Addison Street, a short left detour allows a view of the 1924 *Russian Church (3)*, with its onion domes. ❱ **Continue on Washington Avenue, which becomes Forsyth Street, turning left onto Lafayette Avenue to get to the top of Powderhorn Hill.**

On the right is *Malone Park (4)*, with views over Chelsea from an alley of Scotch pines. ❱ **Turn right onto Summit Avenue; continue past the water tower and turn right onto Crest Avenue.** The buildings of the *Old Soldiers Home and Quigley Hospital (5)* occupy the hilltop. Opened in 1882 to assist Civil War veterans, the home was taken over by the state in 1940. Approximately three hundred veterans are residents. St. Elizabeth Hospital administers the 120-bed hospital and a school for licensed practical nurses. ❱ **Follow Crest Avenue to Clark Avenue; use the stairway to descend to Broadway. (To bypass the stairway, turn right onto Clark Avenue and left onto Eleanor Street.) Turn right, walk two blocks, and turn right again onto Parker Street.**

The *Governor Bellingham/Cary House (6)* is a two-story yellow clapboard farmhouse dating from 1659. Built initially as a hunting lodge, the building was remodeled in the early 1700s. In 1772 the Carys refurbished the house; the English white pine paneling that they added in 1791 is still in place. At an angle to the street, the mansion faces directly south, unlike other nearby homes. Legends of the mansion tell of a possible secret tunnel inside, and a duel on the farm's land. ❱ **Follow Tudor Street southwest, turning left onto Crescent Avenue and then right onto Broadway.**

The *Fitz Memorial Public Library (7)* has a skylit hexagonal atrium. Its fireplace is lined with tiles from the nearby factory of Low Art Tiles, known for high-relief carvings glazed in monochrome tints that pooled in recesses and thinned on elevations to create a feeling of depth. Low's ceramic products

View from Mary O'Malley Park at Mystic River and Tobin Bridge.

were used as paperweights, inkwells, trivets, lamps, flower holders and planters, candlesticks, clock cases, insets for woodstoves, and large ceramic soda fountains.

In *Chelsea Square (8),* longtime Chelsea educator Roman Pucko is remembered in a bronze statue. The park is home to the Chelsea Square Fountain—a monument given by the Polish people to commemorate Casimir Pulaski's help in training colonial cavalry during the revolution. The old post office at 189 Winnisimmet Street replaced offices burned in 1908. During the fire, postal employees saved the mail and sorted it in a nearby billiard parlor. The building now houses the Chelsea Theatreworks, with professional performances, a theater school for adults, training programs for youth, and an exhibition space for local artists. ❱ **Veer left onto Tremont Street, then right onto Medford Street.**

The *Chelsea waterfront (9)* is dominated by gas storage tanks. Near a well-maintained vest-pocket park on Medford Street is a row of late-nineteenth-century, three-story brick town houses that escaped the city's fires. ❱ **Follow Medford Street to Broadway and turn left.**

After World War II a major obstacle to commuter traffic was the Chelsea–Charlestown Bridge, which opened seven thousand times a year for ships on the Mystic River. Eliminating the obstacle, the 2-mile-long *Maurice J. Tobin Bridge (10)* opened in 1950, soaring 254 feet above high tide with an 800-foot main span.

Below the bridge, the lone, two-story building is the Abel Garner House, 28 Broadway, once the *residence of the bridge keeper (11)* for the earlier bridges. The first bridge, opened in 1802, charged a toll until 1869, when the state purchased it and made it free.

Mary O'Malley Park (12) slopes to a seawall at the Mystic River and enhances the former Naval Hospital. At its wharf a compass rose and harbor map are carved in granite. ▶ **At the end of the park, turn right onto Breakwater Drive, and right again on Boatswains Way. Turn left on Captain's Row.**

Facing the Mystic River, the former *Naval Hospital (13)* served from 1836 until 1974, when it was decommissioned. The hospital played a critical role in the 1918 flu epidemic that ravaged the country, leaving more than half a million dead. The best-known patient was Lieutenant John F. Kennedy, treated for wounds received when his PT boat was cut in half in the Pacific war. Nearby was the Marine Hospital, dating from 1827 and burned in 1908. It was replaced by the Shurtleff School, now converted to an early-learning center. All hospital buildings on the hill have now been converted into condominiums.

▶ **At the right of 121 Captain's Row, descend on the stairs to the street under the bridge. Turn right onto Beacon Street. Turn left onto Broadway to return to Bellingham Square.**

Prepared by members of WalkBoston.

walk 15

Dedham

Start and finish: Dedham Square, at Washington and High
    Streets
Getting there: Take the MBTA No. 34 Walpole Center bus
    from Forest Hills MBTA Orange Line Station; the run-
    ning time is 25 minutes, with 15-minute headway on
    weekdays and Saturday and 30-minute headway on
    Sunday
Getting back: Take the MBTA No. 34 bus to Forest Hills
Time: 1½ hours
Distance: Approximately 2.5 miles
Difficulty: Easy; no hills or stairs
Accessibility: Fully wheelchair accessible
Rest rooms: Dedham Police Station in Dedham Square

IN DEDHAM the charm and grace of the early 1800s are still in
evidence. The center of Dedham holds the town's oldest houses
and community buildings and still has bustling activity connected with the Norfolk County Courts. It stands distinct and
removed from other parts of town, where farms became subdi-
visions and local industries once produced everything from
thread to shovels, boots to cigars.

Founded in 1635, Dedham was strategically located on the
great highway of foot, horse, and wagon travel that ran from
Virginia to New Hampshire. Turnpikes, stagecoaches, and

later steam railroads all came through town, bringing prominence and prosperity. Indeed, in its prime Dedham hosted presidents and political leaders, the nation's first free public school, and notable events such as the trial of Sacco and Vanzetti.

The town lost much of its economic primacy before the twentieth century, however, and the automobile hastened its conversion to a suburban community whose boundaries blurred with those of its neighbors. Dedham Square was bypassed by the new Providence Highway (Route 1) in the 1930s. Yet the old center of Dedham still exists, enhanced by the deepened contrast with its surroundings. This walk takes you on a loop around the town's most intriguing sites—an oasis of history in a modern suburb.

🚶 the walk

This walk begins and ends at *Dedham Square (1)*, the intersection of High and Washington Streets. The Dedham Police Station and the local movie house mark the area. Across from the police station is the 1880 brick *Knights of Columbus building (2)*. The site has been occupied since 1638 with a succession of buildings, including residences; a sequence of taverns—Gay's, Polley's, Alden's, and Bride's; and the Phoenix Hotel. ▶ **Head west along High Street.**

The *Dedham Historical Society (3)* occupies the 1888 Romanesque brick building at 612 High Street, on the site of the first post office in Dedham. The land and the money to erect the society's building were donated by the daughter of Jeremiah Shuttleworth, the first postmaster. The society's exhibits include the Metcalf Great Chair, the oldest dated piece of American-made furniture, and many examples of the famed crackle-finished Dedham Pottery, made in the town from 1896 to 1943.

The 1827 *Norfolk County Courthouse (4)*, facing High

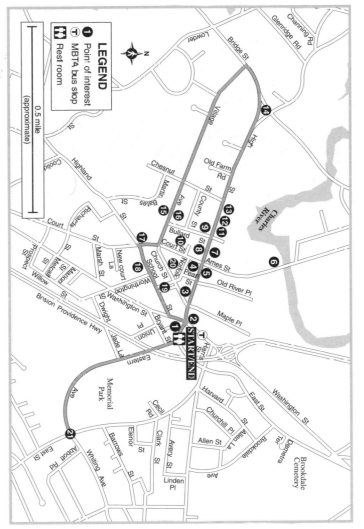

Dedham

Street, has a recognizable tall dome, one of the products of major reconstructions in the 1860s and 1890s. The granite building hosted the trial of Nicola Sacco and Bartolomeo Vanzetti, anarchists alleged to have committed a brutal robbery and murder. Media coverage was extensive; discussions were heavily politicized in an anarchist-hunting atmosphere. For their supporters, the 1927 verdict became a tragedy when Sacco and Vanzetti were sentenced to death in the state's electric chair.

The *Norfolk County Registry of Deeds (5)* occupies the site of the Woodward Tavern, where the County Convention of 1774 met and initiated the drafting of the "Suffolk Resolves" in response to the perceived tyranny of England. ▶ **Follow Ames Street to the right across the Charles River.** From the bridge or on the far riverbank on Pleasant Street is a view of the bucolic setting of the *original town landing (6)* and the "keye" where Dedham's settlers of the late 1630s could safely ford the river. ▶ **Return to High Street and turn right.**

The brick-end mansion on the right is the *Dedham Community House (7)*, built by Samuel Haven in 1795. Abraham Lincoln, who arrived in Dedham to stump for Whig candidates Taylor and Fillmore in 1848, was entertained at a luncheon here.

Across High Street is the *Church Green (8)*, also known as the "Little Common" and the site of the first Norfolk County Courthouse. A granite boulder with a plaque memorializes Dedham's earliest school, the first free public school supported by public taxation in Massachusetts Bay Colony. The Pillar of Liberty was constructed here in 1766, commemorating the repeal of the Stamp Act. It once consisted of a wooden column topped by a bust of William Pitt, who supported the colony in Parliament, but it was destroyed in 1769. The inscribed granite base remains.

Prominently facing the Church Green is the *First Church of Dedham (9)* with its tall spire, built in 1762, and rebuilt in

Court Street, Dedham.

1820, with significant changes through the nineteenth century—but always located on the site where Dedham's earliest church gatherings started with a congregation of eight people in 1638.

Adjacent to Church Green is the *Norfolk House (10)*, 19 Court Street, a large four-story brick house built in 1801 and subsequently used as a tavern and inn. The inn was the center of social, political, and educational activities for Dedham from 1801 to 1865 and a regular stop for some of the stage-coaches that came through town each week. The ballroom of the inn was one of the best in New England. Inn visitors included John Quincy Adams, Andrew Jackson, Martin Van Buren, and Abraham Lincoln. In 1822 an elephant was exhibited here. The inn closed in 1865, when the owners were charged with maintaining a common nuisance. It became a Roman Catholic girls' school and orphanage, then a boarding-house, before it was restored as a residence in 1910.

Across High Street is the 1819 *Congregational Church (11)*. The *Samuel Dexter Mansion (12)* was built in 1765 at 699 High

Street; you can see the mansion by looking along the driveway. An 1845 stone mansion at number 70 Bullard Street is now a day-care center. ❭ **Return to High Street and turn right.**

The *Edward Dowse House (13)* at 700 High Street is set in a large lawn extending to the river. It was built about 1800 by a sea captain and "china merchant" from Boston, who became a congressman during President Monroe's administration; Monroe himself slept here in 1819, during an "Era of Good Feelings" tour of New England.

The *Training Field (14)* dates to 1640. Nearby on Bridge Street was a 1644 cart bridge crossing the Charles River to connect with Dedham Island, nearly surrounded by river and marshes, and the only dry connection to Needham. ❭ **Follow Bridge Street southwest to Village Avenue, and turn left toward Dedham Center.**

Opposite Bullard Street is the *First Parish Cemetery (15)*, set apart in 1636; the earliest burials are found to the left of the entrance. Here lie the founders of the town, although the oldest standing stone dates only to 1678. The dark building opposite the cemetery is the former *Norfolk County House of Correction (16)*, now converted to residential condominiums. The building, designed in 1850 by Gridley J. F. Bryant, a prominent Boston architect, was built with granite facades and arched Gothic windows.

At the corner of Court Street is the 1859 *St. Paul's Episcopal Church (17)*—the fourth church building erected by that group. The stone tower, suffering from vibrations caused by traffic on the street, was taken down, stone by stone, and re-erected in 1929. ❭ **Turn right onto Court Street, then left onto School Street.**

The interesting houses on *School Street (18)* include No. 72, built in 1818 with an attached workshop for a blacksmith. In 1822 the town built the Center School at 61–63 School Street. The school's bell tower was removed in 1859 and the building converted into a two-family dwelling.

From 1798 until 1845 *Franklin Square (19)* was the site of the second Episcopal church building. Some nearby buildings occupy land bequeathed to the Episcopal Church "for their use forever" and pay land rent to the church under 999-year leases.

At Norfolk and Church Streets is the *Dedham Public Library (20)*, a Romanesque stone building erected in 1888. Note the stone checkerboard on the gable.

Ambitious walkers may want to extend the walk from here to visit the 1637 *Fairbanks House (21)* on East Street, recognized as the oldest wooden frame house in the country. The Fairbanks family has owned the house for more than three hundred years. ▶ **From Dedham Square follow Eastern Avenue southeast for about a third of a mile, crossing Route 1 very carefully and passing a park to reach the modest house.**

Prepared by members of WalkBoston.

 **walk 16**

East Cambridge and Kendall Square

Start: Lechmere Station, MBTA Green Line outbound platform
Getting there: Take the MBTA Green Line to Lechmere Station
Finish: Kendall Square Station, MBTA Red Line
Getting back: Take the MBTA Red Line at Kendall Square
Time: 2 hours
Distance: Approximately 3 miles
Difficulty: Easy
Accessibility: Fully wheelchair accessible
Rest rooms: Middlesex County Courthouses

FOR URBAN CONTRASTS, this is the walk. The small industrial-courthouse town that once was East Cambridge is now ringed with new and reused buildings that house high-tech and other office-based firms. The high-rise buildings around Kendall Square announce the arrival of a center of activities and businesses closely connected with the Massachusetts Institute of Technology. A huge nearby enclosed mall looms over the local business area. The contrast between the relatively sleepy East Cambridge community and the job-focused business centers around it could not be more dramatic.

The contrast was there from the beginning. In 1810 specula-

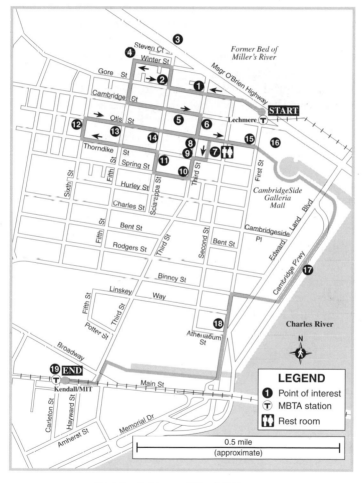

East Cambridge and Kendall Square

tor Andrew Craigie envisioned a community on an island cut off by salt marshes from the Charles River in the east part of Cambridge. He built a new bridge to connect his island to Boston, laid out a grid of streets, and began attracting development to his advantageous location midway between downtown Boston and Old Cambridge (Harvard Square). He even constructed a courthouse in an attempt to convince Middlesex County to relocate its judiciary here. (It worked.)

East Cambridge quickly became a center of heavy manufacturing, producing everything from soap to scientific instruments; you will pass by several former industrial sites on this walk. In the twentieth century, however, the riverfront was beautified: Science Park Dam replaced the Canal Bridge, traffic was diverted onto new boulevards, and old industrial buildings were renovated as offices. New pedestrian routes were built to link residential, employment, and recreation areas to the Charles River. In short, the neighborhood came to embody the modern urban vision.

Today this distinctive and modest community is located within a convenient pedestrian radius of neighboring areas where construction activity is booming—Kendall Square, with its new offices, and North Point, where high-rise residences face the Charles River. Within this walk's few brief miles you'll visit the best of Cambridge, past and present.

the walk

▶ **To begin the walk, head west on Gore Street to its intersection with Third Street.** The *First Houses (1)*—two of the earliest houses in East Cambridge—were built before 1820 by Andrew Craigie's company. Craigie lured residents with easy credit for construction and by giving out free passes over his toll bridge. ▶ **Continue on Gore Street, turning right onto Sciarappa Street and then left onto Winter Street.**

Workers' housing (2) in the area north of Cambridge Street contains a full range of spec-built homes—from Georgian-Federal buildings to early-twentieth-century tenements—along Gore and Winter Streets.

Glass and coffin companies and slaughterhouses (3) were located near Bridge Street (now O'Brien Highway). Early glass manufacturers concentrated at Miller's River. The Lockhart coffin factory (now an antiques mall) faced Bridge Street. Nine slaughterhouses lined Miller's River; the largest plant, Squire's (processing 350,000 hogs a year), was located at Gore and Seventh Streets.

Near Squire's slaughterhouse, the *Meigs Railroad (4)*, one of the first monorails in the country, was built in 1885 on a monorail test track. Cylindrical steam-powered trains were held aloft by a row of posts, each holding two rails, one mounted above the other. The advent of electricity led to its demise. ▶ **Turn left onto Fifth Street; at Cambridge Street, turn left.**

Along the walk are many commercial buildings used by businesses of East Cambridge. One of the most unusual is the *East Cambridge Savings Bank (5)*, a locally based firm in a building enlarged with flair in 1976. Its expansion and new facade were created by using a bay of the existing building. In the courthouse yard at Cambridge and Third Streets, *History Corner (6)* contains a detailed series of maps to orient visitors to East Cambridge. ▶ **Turn right onto Third Street.**

The *Middlesex County Courthouses (7)* provided an early focus for East Cambridge, as developer Andrew Craigie correctly assumed when he persuaded the county commissioners to accept his offer of land and a courthouse. To demonstrate his serious intent, Craigie hired the prestigious Charles Bulfinch to design the first building. The original 1814 Bulfinch courthouse hides within the 1848 courthouse—restored in 1986 and called *Bulfinch Square*. The 1889 *Clerk of Courts Building* was built to accommodate the burgeoning Probate Court. The *Registry of Deeds and Probate Court* is a

Thordike Street houses, Cambridge.

monumental building of 1896 that boasts four giant brick-columned porticoes and steep flights of stairs. The *New Superior Court Building* is a twenty-two-story building that replaced the former Middlesex County jail and power plant in 1982. Mismanagement of construction and enormous cost overruns led to a reversal of demolition orders on the older court buildings nearby. The *Third District Court,* across Third Street, is a two-story Georgian Revival built in 1931. ▶ **Walk**

behind the Bulfinch Building and return to Third Street, continuing south. Note the houses facing the courthouses.

Third Street's *Quality Row (8)* is a row of houses dating to 1860; mansard roofs and high stoops catered to tastes of the gentry. Connected to Quality Row, *Holy Cross Polish Church (9)* is an 1827 building that retains its original broad entrance tower and recessed window arches. Behind the church at 59 Thorndike Street is a tall 1827 Georgian brick house with a side garden and an unusual fence. ❯ **Turn right onto Spring Street.**

A frame row at 67 Spring Street occupies the *site of the house of Thomas Graves (10)*, the first settler of East Cambridge in the seventeenth century. ❯ **Turn right onto Sciarappa Street, then left onto Thorndike Street.**

Several *Thorndike Street houses (11)* warrant special attention. At 74 Thorndike Street is an unusual T-shaped Greek Revival house with two-story openwork corner pillars. A front garden faces 85 Thorndike Street, an 1822 center-hall house, later embellished with brackets and a projecting entrance bay. No. 96 is the 1826 residence of Cambridge mayor James Green, a side-hall house with a brick front, arched entrance recess, and wooden fanlight in the gable. ❯ **Walk to the bottom of the hill and turn right onto Sixth Street.**

Sacred Heart Church (12) is an imposing 1874 Victorian Gothic church of blue slate with granite trim. ❯ **Turn right onto Otis Street.** Starting at the church, the walk climbs past interesting *Otis Street houses (13)*. The *Putnam School (14)* of 1887 occupies the site of Revolutionary Fort Putnam, built by George Washington in 1775; it became residences in 1983. ❯ **Pass through the courthouse area and cross Second Street.**

At the once tidal site where the British landed en route to Lexington in 1775, the *Davenport/Irving & Casson buildings (15)* illustrate the furniture industry dominance of part of East Cambridge in the 1860s. The Davenport Company was known for a popular sofa design.

Pedestrian ways on Otis and Thorndike Streets link to the riverfront through the *Lechmere Triangle (16)*. Dramatic shopping, residences, and offices occupy a former industrial site. A 60-foot fountain spouts from the reconstructed Lechmere Canal, originally built in 1874 for industrial shipping. ❱ **Follow Otis Street to the walkway around the fountain.**

As the canal nears the Charles River, a path leads under Land Boulevard. The *Front at the Charles River (17)* is a major pedestrian area on the Charles River, from the Science Museum to the Longfellow Bridge, following a design originated by the Olmsted landscape architects. The Front is a good vantage point to see downtown Boston and the landmark Longfellow Bridge. ❱ **Turn right along the river. Turn right at the park that leads to Binney Street. Follow Binney to First Street, and turn left.**

The *Athanaeum Press and Carter's Ink Buildings (18)* became the first industrial buildings in the area renovated for modern offices, in 1981. Just beyond the power plant is the Broad Canal, laid out in 1806; the walkway alongside was built in 1986. ❱ **Follow the canal west to Third Street. Turn left, then right onto Main Street.**

In the *Kendall Square area (19)*, Point Park holds a sculpture with water features created by artist Otto Piene. Diagonally across Third Street from the park is the U.S. Volpe Transportation Systems Center building, originally intended for NASA research facilities. Walk from the park along Main Street through the heart of the area, a high-rise community clustering around M.I.T. ❱ **The walk ends at the MBTA Red Line Subway Station in Kendall Square.**

ROBERT SLOANE, *a lawyer and city planner, serves as Walks Chair for WalkBoston.*

 **walk 17**

Lexington

Start: Arlington Heights bus station
Getting there: Take the MBTA No. 77/79 bus from the Harvard Square Red Line Station
Finish: Battle Green in Lexington Center
Getting back: Take the MBTA No. 62/76 bus to Alewife Red Line Station or Lexpress local buses to the town line near the Arlington Heights station
Time: 4 hours
Distance: 5 miles
Difficulty: Easy
Accessibility: Fully wheelchair accessible
Rest rooms: Visitor center near Buckman Tavern

THE EXTRAORDINARY EVENTS of April 19, 1775, took place along a single dirt road between Boston, Lexington, and Concord. British troops, whose leaders were convinced that colonists had stores of arms in the area, planned to march on this road from Boston. Paul Revere and William Dawes set up an early-warning system and traveled this road before dawn—and before the British set out—to alert colonists. Colonial Minutemen, forewarned by Revere and Dawes, hurried to Lexington on this road to confront the approaching British. The "shots heard 'round the world" were fired early in the morning on a spring day in Lexington. Actions later in

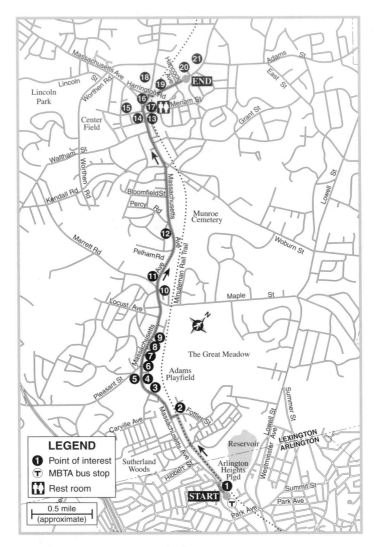

Lexington

the afternoon further demonstrated the commitment of the colonists: as the British troops retreated from Concord and Lexington toward Boston, they were fired upon by Minutemen lurking behind trees and stone walls lining the fields along this road. On that day the American Revolution began.

This road is now the route of a fascinating walk through Revolutionary history. As you stroll in and near beautiful Lexington, you'll visit the sites of troop movements, skirmishes, and battles. The walk's centerpiece, the Lexington Battle Green, is lined with many of the original buildings that witnessed the opening of the war. Interspersed among historic sites along the way are nineteenth- and twentieth-century buildings that reflect Lexington's development into a commercial center, and then a livable suburb. The former dirt road is now wide, modern Massachusetts Avenue, which would be unrecognizable to the early colonists. Still, the town known as "Birthplace of American Liberty" retains a leafy and open quality that welcomes walkers.

🚶 the walk

▶ **Leave the Arlington Heights bus station, turn right, and look for the entrance to the Minuteman Rail-Trail near the drugstore.** ▶ **Begin your walk heading north-northwest on the Minuteman Rail-Trail (1).**

This popular bikeway was built in 1993 on the former route of the Lexington & West Cambridge Railroad of 1846. A parallel streetcar service and, later, buses reduced demand for the railroad; it was abandoned in 1977.

The site of the *East Lexington Train station (2)* and Cutler's Tavern were late-1800s landmarks in an unsavory part of town, with cockfights in the woods, card games, and liberally served alcohol. Massachusetts Avenue was dubbed "Hell Street" because it led to perdition in East Lexington. ▶ **Exit the rail-trail via Fottler Avenue (the second street to** cross the rail-trail). Continue north-northwest, now on Massachusetts Avenue.

On the right side of the avenue, *Robbins Cemetery (3)* contains the graves of the prominent family that founded East Lexington and brought prosperity by establishing a local fur industry. Just beyond, a small cluster of buildings marks the center of East Lexington. The *Morell-Dana House (4)*, a cottage built in 1803, became a prominent Greek Revival monument with the 1849 addition of pillars, a porch, and a second floor. Across the street the *Brown Farmhouse (5)*, 620 Massachusetts Avenue, was the center of a 100-acre farm in the eighteenth century; its acreage is now occupied by Wilson Farms, a popular produce market. The *Old Brick store (6)*, built by Stephen Robbins in 1828, housed a grocery and post office on the first floor, and a meeting hall above. Down the street is the 1833 *Stone Building (7)*, built by the Robbins family as a lecture and meeting hall during the abolitionist period before the Civil War. A gift from the Stone family in 1892 transformed it into the East Branch Public Library.
▶ **Continue down Massachusetts Avenue.**

The *Follen Community Church (9)* was built to follow a notion circulating in the 1840s that an octagon shape closely resembled a sphere, and was thus a form found in nature. The shape also had practical advantages: it provided more space and was easier to heat. At one time, Ralph Waldo Emerson preached here.

Taking advantage of its main road location, the *Bowen Tavern (9)*, 881 Massachusetts Avenue, catered to teamsters and farmers driving sheep, turkeys, and cattle to Brighton slaughterhouses between 1825 and 1845. It was one of twelve taverns lining the old dirt road in that era to slake farmers' thirst.

The 1716 *Stephen Robbins House (10)*, 1295 Massachusetts Avenue, was built by a prominent member of the Robbins family and later occupied by Ellen Stone, a lawyer and the

FREDERICA MATERA

Minuteman statue, Lexington Green, Lexington.

public benefactor who donated the East Branch library. Stone was known as an eccentric who defied the town by cutting down street trees.

At the intersection of Massachusetts Avenue and Marrett Road, the *Museum of Our National Heritage (11)* highlights American history with changing exhibits of memorabilia, including coin banks, tavern and inn signs, banjos and clocks, toys, furniture, and costumes.

Built in the 1690s, *Munroe Tavern (12)* became headquarters and field hospital for the British in their retreat after the Concord and Lexington battles. George Washington, visiting the battle sites after the war, dined here. ◗ **Massachusetts Avenue now brings you into the heart of Lexington.**

Here the *Old Train Station (13)* faces Emery Park (formerly Depot Square). This 1847 landmark greeted passengers on eighteen daily trains to and from Boston. Now owned by the Lexington Historical Society, the building is becoming a museum.

Just before the town green is the *Cary Memorial Library (14)*, built in 1906 using funds supplied by Maria Hastings Cary to expand the 1827 Juvenile Library. In its early years only those younger than fourteen could borrow books, and then only one at a time. The 1886 *Dawn of Liberty* painting hangs inside, thanks to $3,100 raised by the Lexington Historical Society. ❱ **Turn left on Clarke Street for one block**.

At the *Old Belfry (15)*—originally built in 1762—bells rang out to warn citizens of the oncoming British. The present belfry is a 1910 reconstruction. ❱ **Return to Massachusetts Avenue**.

The most important historic site in Lexington is *Battle Green (16)*. Here, on the morning of April 19, 1775, two long lines of Captain Parker's Minutemen faced the approaching British. Of the seventy-seven colonists participating, eight Minutemen died and ten were wounded; two British soldiers were wounded. Look for the *Minuteman Statue*, created with a gift from railroad lawyer and state senator Francis Hayes and unveiled in 1900. The Hayes Memorial Water Fountain, below the statue, is now filled with flowers. Nearby is the *Revolutionary Monument*, marking a burial spot for battle casualties. Dedicated in 1799, it is the oldest war memorial in the country.

Across Massachusetts Avenue is the *Buckman Tavern (17)*, built in 1709. This was the meeting place for dozens of Minutemen just prior to the battle on April 19, 1775. Its original 7-foot-wide taproom fireplace, bar, and bullet-scarred front door remain.

Facing the green is the *First Parish Church (18)* on the site of the first church of Cambridge Farms, built here in 1692. Behind it is the old 1690s Burying Ground. Look for the graves of Captain Parker and others, including a British soldier killed in the battle.

Lexington Academy (19), a private grammar school started in 1823, later became a "normal" school for teacher training.

The town equipped the school with two stoves, two maps, a pair of gloves, and about a hundred books. It is now the Masonic Hall. ▌ **Follow Hancock Street north from the green for a quarter mile.**

The *Hancock-Clarke House (20),* where John Hancock and Sam Adams rested on April 18, 1775, was the destination of Dawes and Revere on their midnight rides to warn of the approaching British troops. The *Antique Fire Equipment Museum (21),* in a barn behind the Hancock-Clarke House, displays nozzles, leather hoses and hose carts, paper tape alarm systems, and Lexington's first motorized fire engine.

▌ **Return to the Battle Green to end the walk.**

LISA BRYANT *is a longtime Lexington resident and an avid AMC hiker.*

 **walk 18**

Newton Upper Falls

Start: MBTA Eliot Station on the Green Line Riverside
Branch
Getting there: Take the MBTA Green Line D Train out-
bound from stations in Boston or Brookline, or inbound
from Riverside Station
Finish: MBTA Waban Station or Eliot Station on the
MBTA Green Line
Getting back: Return via the Riverside MBTA Green Line
from Waban Station or return to Eliot Station via the
sidewalk on Route 9
Time: 2 hours
Distance: About 3 miles
Difficulty: Moderate
Accessibility: Fully wheelchair accessible
Rest rooms: No public rest rooms

A HIDDEN MILL VILLAGE on the Charles River, Newton Upper
Falls is tucked into a busy corner of the metropolitan area.
On this walk you will see a potpourri of eighteenth- and
nineteenth-century architecture, many charming hilly and
curving streets, and a major National Historic Landmark—
Echo Bridge over the Charles River's Hemlock Gorge.

Upper Falls was settled at the largest falls on the Charles
River—a drop of 26 feet over a few hundred feet of its length.

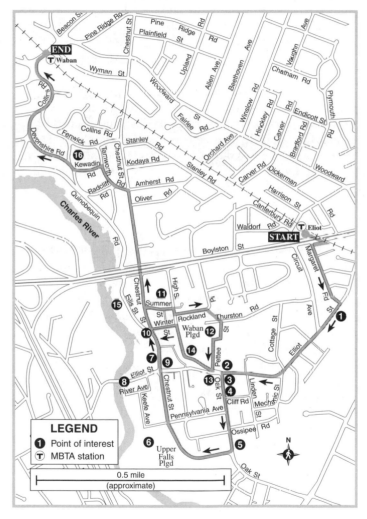

Newton Upper Falls

Native Americans discovered the falls and established fish weirs here to harvest eels and other freshwater fish. In 1688 John Clark bought rights to build at the falls from Chief Nahatan for £12 sterling. By 1813, when a cotton mill was installed, industrial buildings lined the gorge from the falls area to the newly built Worcester Turnpike (now Route 9). Within forty years a quarter of Newton's population lived and worked in Upper Falls. Today a large portion of the village is protected as a designated historic district. Of the 150 buildings that existed a hundred years ago in Upper Falls, 118 still stand. This walk is designed to touch a sampling of these antique buildings—industrial, civic, and residential—offering a firsthand view of the fabric of an early-nineteenth-century settlement.

the walk

▶ **Leave the MBTA Eliot Station via the Route 9 footbridge, turn right onto Route 9, then turn left onto Margaret Road. At Elliot Street, turn right; the road will soon bend due west.**

Eliot Station was named for John Eliot, the seventeenth-century minister who preached to the Native Americans living in the area. *Elliot Street (1)* was named for Simon Elliot, who founded the Elliot Manufacturing Company in Upper Falls in 1782. One of the oldest in Upper Falls, Elliot Street was the main connection to the rest of Newton and to Boston until construction of the Worcester Turnpike (Route 9). It's lined with cottages built for workers in the mills during the early to mid-1800s and a large boardinghouse for mill workers at Mechanic Street.

At the corner of Oak Street is the *Stone Institute (2)*, a home for elders in Sunnyside; it was originally the nineteenth-century house of Otis Pettee, a mill superintendent for the Elliots and later owner of the mills. Pettee built the village post office, school, and church as well as housing for the mill workers and their families. He founded the Charles River Railroad, which ran through the village. Also look for the 1909 *Mary Immaculate of Lourdes Roman Catholic Church (3)* on the corner, with its 1838 Greek Revival parish house next door. ▌**Turn left onto Oak Street.**

At Cliff Road is a stone cottage and a large *stone barn (4)* built in 1839 by Otis Pettee. The barn is renowned from its appearances in the *Ripley's Believe It or Not* newspaper features as the country's only four-story building with a ground entrance on every floor, an achievement of ingenious site grading. A magnificent copper beech tree more than 150 years old stands on the opposite side of Oak Street.

The intersection of Oak and Chestnut Streets is called *Pettee Square (5)*. Its main feature is the original Upper Falls railroad depot on Pettee's Charles River Railroad. Many trainloads of gravel were carried on this track in the 1850s to create the landfill in Boston's Back Bay. ▌**Turn right onto Chestnut Street, a major thoroughfare of the old mill district. Chestnut will soon veer due north.**

You pass a small commercial center, more old houses, and a *baseball field (6)* where the baseball immortal Satchel Paige is said to have pitched at a barnstorming semipro game in the 1940s. You can also see one of the 1,000-foot transmission towers clustered in the area.

At Elliot Street are what remains of *Elliot Mills (7)*, founded on the site of John Clark's 1688 sawmill powered by the falls of the Charles River. The mill was enlarged in 1823 by Simon Elliott III and Thomas Handesyde Perkins, a well-known Boston capitalist and philanthropist. It continued to grow under Otis Pettee's leadership, producing not only textiles but also cotton-processing machinery designed by Pettee and shipped to other mills. Converted to silk manufacturing after the Civil War, the mill remained in operation until the 1960s.

Take a look at the nearby *Elliot Street Bridge (8)* over the Charles River: a mortarless stone arch structure that's more than two hundred years old. Several *historic houses (9)* on both Elliot and Chestnut Streets near this intersection date to as early as 1785. Dr. Joseph Warren, a resident of Upper Falls in the 1840s who became Abraham Lincoln's personal physician, had his office here, at 344 Elliot Street. Other buildings were moved to their sites to give land to the expanding mill, including the odd half-Cape house opposite the mill. ◗ **Continue north up Chestnut Street past the mills.**

The *old Town Center (10)*, adjacent to the mills, includes an 1832 Baptist church, an old general store (now offices), and a row of 1830s–1850s commercial buildings. ◗ **Proceed along Chestnut Street to Summer Street and turn right.**

In the *1828 church (11)* Ralph Waldo Emerson preached on two occasions. ◗ **Jog right on High Street and then left to walk east up narrow Rockland Place, entering a dirt pathway at the bend in the road.** The pathway emerges at a playground. Here the large Victorian *Emerson School (12)*, built in 1904, was converted to condominiums around 1980. ◗ **Walk south down Pettee Street to Elliot Street.**

At the corner of High, Oak, and Elliot Streets was the *terminus of the 1892 Newton and Boston Street Railway (13)*. This line contributed to the development of Boston's western streetcar suburbs until it was replaced by buses in 1932. ◗ **Veer right onto High Street.** At an overlook a fine Stick-style house can be seen. On High Street is a *collection of houses (14)* from the 1830s to 1850s in a variety of architectural styles, particularly Greek Revival. ◗ **Turn left on Winter Street, completing a loop, and carefully cross Chestnut Street. Turn right onto Chestnut and follow it one block to Summer Street.**

Opposite Summer is a footpath just to the right of a large brick building and another storefront. On the path is *Echo Bridge (15)*, once one of America's largest masonry arch structures, with a 130-foot central span. It was built in 1876 by Boston Water Works (note the BWW insignia on railings) to

BOB BERGMAN, MARKETING IMAGES

Echo Bridge, Newton Upper Falls.

support the aqueduct from the Sudbury Reservoirs to Boston. The bridge spans Hemlock Gorge, an MDC reservation. From the bridge there is a good view of the Elliot Mills and the outlet through which water rejoined the river after turning millwheels. A popular amusement park with a dance pavilion once stood on the bluff above the falls. (**Warning:** Although an echo can be heard by standing under the bridge, footing under the bridge is very hazardous.)

▶ Return to Chestnut Street, turn left , and walk down the hill, passing more workers' cottages from the 1830s and leaving Upper Falls. At Route 9, there are two options for your return. You can retrace your route to the Eliot MBTA station by turning right and following Route 9 until you see the MBTA overpass and pedestrian bridge to Eliot Station. Or you can follow the pleasant residential streets of Waban. From Chestnut Street, turn left onto Tamworth Road, then left again on Kewadin Road; follow Devonshire Road north to Collins Road and Beacon Street.

This *hundred-year-old subdivision (16)* in Waban was laid

out on principles developed by the eminent landscape architect Frederick Law Olmsted. It was a result of the land boom that followed the extension of the Highland Branch commuter railroad to Waban in 1886.

▶ **End your walk at Waban Village, where the MBTA Waban Station is located.**

JAMES PURDY *is a resident of Newton Upper Falls and a planning consultant at Wallace Floyd Design Group.*

walk 19

Wakefield

Start and finish: At the intersection of Wakefield's Main
  Street and Water Street
Getting there: Take the MBTA Orange Line to Oak Grove;
  the No. 136 or 137 bus to Wakefield; or the Commuter
  Rail Line from North Station
Getting back: Take the No. 136 or 137 bus to Oak Grove; or
  the Commuter Rail Line to North Station
Time: 2½ hours
Distance: 3.5 miles
Difficulty: Easy
Accessibility: Fully wheelchair accessible
Rest rooms: Town hall; public library

WAKEFIELD is an attractive, breezy town overlooking Lake
Quannapowitt, a favorite of boaters and sailboarders. On the
perimeter of Route 128, the town feels more like a self-
sustained commercial center than a typical suburb. Once a
prosperous center manufacturing wicker, cane, and rattan
products, Wakefield has now arranged its downtown buildings
into a civic center of churches, public buildings, and parkland
on the banks of the lake. Several ancient restored houses rein-
force the fact that Wakefield is in fact a very old community—
indeed, it was first settled by Europeans in 1639.

The town was dramatically changed when Cyrus Wakefield

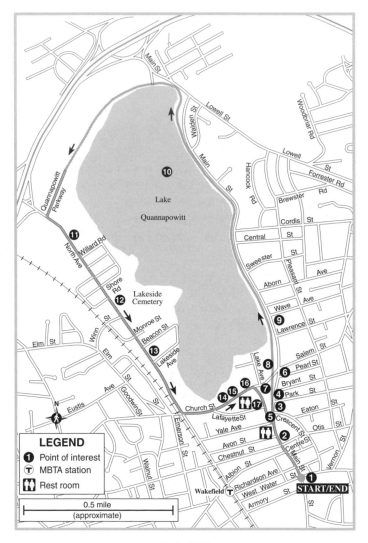

Wakefield

moved from Boston in 1851, relocating and enlarging his phenomenally successful Wakefield Rattan Company, which popularized the use of wicker in the United States. His financial success led him into philanthropy. When he offered to build the community a new town hall in 1868, the town renamed itself for him. After he died in 1873 the company remained successful for decades but finally closed its doors in 1930.

These days technology industries have replaced manufacturing. This walk explores the community's ancient center and winds around lovely Lake Quannapowitt to return to its beginning. It is a loop both tranquil and historic.

🚶 the walk

▶ **From its intersection with Water Street, walk north on Main Street toward the town center.** *Main Street (1)* was a Native American trail until 1651. In the early town a narrow common extended to the lake from this wide thoroughfare. The *Wakefield Building (2)* at 414–416 Main, was built about 1870 by Cyrus Wakefield to encourage new businesses. The well-built, mansard-style civic facility is a symbol of the economic prosperity that the entrepreneur brought to town.

The oldest church building in town is the *Universalist Unitarian Church (3),* at 326 Main. Constructed in 1836 in the Greek Revival style, it was radically altered to the Italianate style in 1856. The *Benjamin Wiley House (4),* at 316 Main, was built in the Federal style in 1822 by a shoemaker. During the 1830s rooms on the third floor were rented out to students at the Baptist South Reading Academy, the town's first institution of higher learning.

In the center of Main Street is the *Rockery (5),* constructed in 1884 as a "sylvan grotto" to ornament Main Street. The *Hiker* statue, by Theodore Kitson, was added in 1926 to honor soldiers who fought in the Spanish-American War.

The *Emmanuel Parish Church (6)* at Main and Bryant Streets was built circa 1881 in the Stick and Tudor Revival styles. It's now the home of the Episcopal Society, with an attached Parish House on Bryant Street.

A triangular stretch of land, the *Upper Common (7)* is the home of a number of veterans' memorials, the most prominent of which is the *Soldiers and Sailors Memorial* by Harriet Flint, built in 1902 to honor Civil War veterans. Nearer the lake, the *Lower Common (8)* was added in 1885 thanks in part to the generosity of Cornelius Sweetser, a Saco, Maine, resident who left a bequest to be used for public parklands. The town bandstand on the common, once called the Pagoda, has a distinctive Queen Anne form and prominent lakeside location that have made it a town symbol. ❱ **Continue north on Main Street.**

The *Main Street residential area (9)* follows Lake Quannopowitt's eastern shore. The *Eaton House,* 252 Main, is a brick Federal design, constructed about 1818 and notable for the murals on the dining room walls painted by Rufus Porter, an itinerant interior decorator. The Queen Anne–style 1888 *Wright House,* 202 Main, is now a nursing home. No. 194, the *William White House,* is a Greek Revival home built circa 1850 for a prominent family in the shoe industry. The *Young House,* No. 190, is a robust example of Italianate architecture, lavishly remodeled in the 1870s and 1880s by a Boston grocery firm executive. No. 142, the 1798 *Beebe-Brown House,* was modeled on Salem's mansions. The *Stimpson House,* 114 Main Street, was built before 1750 in the Georgian/Federal style on a large farm. ❱ **Walk counterclockwise around Lake Quannapowitt, roughly 3 miles, mostly at lakeside.**

Lake Quannapowitt (10), called the Great Pond by early settlers, has always been important to the town. Its fertile shores, cleared by the Native Americans, were attractive to the first European settlers. It was renamed in the 1840s for James Quonopohit, a Native American. The 264-acre lake

FREDERICA MATERA

Old 1689 Burying Ground, Wakefield.

has a history of industrial ice-harvesting as well as recreational uses—from swimming to skating, boating, and sailboarding. The steamboat *Minni Mariah* plied its waters in the 1870s; boathouses still rent canoes and rowboats. ▶ **Leave the lakeside path via Quannapowitt Parkway.**

On the far side of Lake Quannapowitt, *North Avenue (11)*

was first known as Grove Street for the "pleasure groves" along the lake; because it paralleled the railroad, it later became known as Railroad Avenue. The railroad and North Avenue were sites of icehouses storing the ice harvested from Lake Quannapowitt. ▶ **Turn left. Walk down North Avenue toward the town center.**

Lakeside Cemetery (12) is the resting place of many of the town's notable nineteenth-century residents, with interesting marble and granite monuments. *Temple Israel Cemetery (13),* at Beacon Street, was established about 1860 by Boston's Temple Israel, Boston's first synagogue. ▶ **Turn left onto Church Street.** One of the oldest structures in town, the *Hartshorne House (14),* constructed in 1681, was home for many years to a prominent shoe manufacturer. Now owned by the town of Wakefield, it's maintained by a nonprofit organization. *Church Street* contains a cluster of some of Wakefield's oldest surviving homes, including Nos. 46 (1814), 44 (1790), 42 (1800), 40 (1804), 38 (1803), and 34 (1812).

Significant examples of Puritan gravestone art can be found at the *Old 1689 Burying Ground (15).* Historical markers lead you on a tour. ▶ **Turn right onto Common Street.**

A *striking group of public and ecclesiastical buildings (16)* lines the west side of the common. At the corner of Lafayette Street, the 1912 *First Parish Congregational Church,* a handsome Richardsonian Romanesque stone church, is the fifth meetinghouse of the congregation. Built as the town's high school in high Italianate style in 1871, *Wakefield Town Hall,* 1 Lafayette Street, was altered by WPA workers in the 1930s, who recast it as a neoclassical building. The *First Baptist Church,* at Lafayette and Common Streets, is in the Italianate style so prominent among Wakefield's churches. The church stands next to the YMCA, built by subscription in 1908. The *post office,* built in 1936, is a high-level example of twentieth-century civic architecture. Next door is the *Beebe Memorial*

Library, designed by Ralph Adams Cram and completed in 1923. Its benefactor was Lucius Beebe; his grandson, also named Lucius Beebe, traveled the country in elaborate private railroad cars and was known as a bon vivant for his wit, extravagant style, and gourmet taste. He wrote thirty books, many on the topic of railroad history.

The *Oddfellows Building (17)*, 349–353 Main Street, was constructed in the Renaissance Revival style in 1895 by furniture dealer John Flanley. Saved from imminent demolition after a disastrous fire, it is now part of the Savings Bank, chartered in 1869 with Cyrus Wakefield as its president. The bank's Main Street Clock, constructed in 1902, is a local landmark.

▶ **Turn right from Main Street onto Chestnut Street for the commuter rail station one long block down. Stay on Main Street for bus service.**

NANCY BERTRAND *chairs the Wakefield Historical Commission.*

West Cambridge

Start and finish: Harvard Square MBTA Red Line Station
Getting there: Take the MBTA Red Line or bus service to
  Harvard Square
Getting back: Return on the MBTA Red Line or bus service
Time: 3 hours
Distance: Approximately 4 miles
Difficulty: Easy; all major streets are signalized
Accessibility: Partially wheelchair accessible
Rest rooms: Harvard Coop; Holyoke Center in Harvard
  Square; Mount Auburn Cemetery

THE PATHWAYS OF CAMBRIDGE spread far beyond its famous education centers. Some areas, such as the Charles River, are well known to present and former students. Still, the secrets of the leafy residential areas west of Harvard Square are likely to remain unseen until teased out by a journey on foot with an advisory text in hand.

Cambridge was founded in 1630 by English colonists seeking opportunity and religious freedom. Much of the street pattern dates from colonial times, though of course the river has now been tamed and is no longer tidal.

Close to Harvard Square, limited amounts of land, combined with population increases, have resulted in low buildings being replaced by high-rise structures of late. Most of the

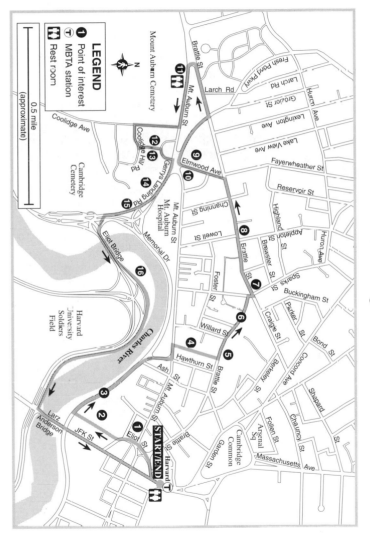

West Cambridge

LEGEND

1 Point of interest
Ⓣ MBTA station
Rest room

0.5 mile
(approximate)

N

Mount Auburn Cemetery

Coolidge Ave

Brattle St

Larch Rd

Fresh Pond Pkwy

Larch Rd

Huron Ave

Groz(or) St

Lexington Ave

Lake View Ave

Mt. Auburn St

Coolidge Hill Rd

Cambridge Cemetery

Gerrys Landing Rd

Elmwood Ave

Fayerwheather St

Reservoir St

Channing St

Highland

Appleton St

Huron Ave

Mt. Auburn St

Mt. Auburn Hospital

Lowell St

Brattle

Brewster St

Memorial Dr

Eliot Bridge

Foster St

Sparks St

Buckingham St

Craigie St

Parker St

Bond St

Harvard University Soldiers Field

Charles River

Willard St

Brattle St

Berkeley St

Concord Ave

Shepard St

Hawthorn St

Ash St

Mt. Auburn St

Cambridge Common

Garden St

Follen St

Chauncy St

St

Arsenal Sq

Larz Anderson Bridge

JFK St

Eliot St

Brattle St

Harvard

START/END

Massachusetts Ave

areas included in this walk, however, have been protected as historic districts for many years; even earlier, their national importance discouraged demolition and radical architectural changes.

The Charles River itself is lined with parks of varying widths along its banks and provides elegant and obvious walking opportunities. It is a popular spot for recreational boating—principally rowing and sailing. The Metropolitan District Commission has the dual role of maintaining the parks and of moving the traffic along the roadway edging the park. In this competition, the parkland is somewhat squeezed.

As a whole West Cambridge presents many contrasts of natural beauty and architectural landmarks. The quality of the built environment is exceptionally high. Landscaping is mature and well maintained. Views vary from close-up to several miles. The Brattle Street and Coolidge Hill neighborhoods and Mount Auburn Cemetery are enclaves, quiet and distinct, yet very close to Harvard Square. This tour through one of Boston's most exquisite neighborhoods will reveal its marvels—known and unknown.

🚶 the walk

▶ **From Harvard Square, follow Brattle Street to Eliot Street.** Harvard University's Kennedy School of Government and the Charles Hotel are major landmarks of *Charles Square (1)*. Between them, a walkway leads to *John F. Kennedy Park (2)*. Inscriptions taken from President Kennedy's speeches are incised on granite entrance posts. ▶ **Turn right onto Memorial Drive (3), built in 1896, and walk beneath the overarching sycamore trees. Then turn right onto Hawthorn Street, jogging briefly left onto Mount Auburn Street.**

Longfellow Park (4) is the "view corridor" between the Charles River and the Vassall-Craigie-Longfellow House.

WALK3OSTON STAFF

Longfellow House, Cambridge.

The lower park contains a 1914 bust of Henry Wadsworth Longfellow by Daniel Chester French, separated from the upper park by ten stone steps. ▶ **Climb the stairs (these can be avoided via Hawthorne Street). The upper park extends to Brattle Street.**

The High Georgian–style *Vassall-Craigie-Longfellow House (5)* at 105 Brattle Street was built in 1759 by John Vassal, a British sympathizer; the structure was confiscated during the Revolution and became the headquarters of General George Washington during the British siege of Boston. Owner Andrew Craigie was the developer of East

Cambridge. A later resident was Henry Wadsworth Longfellow, one of the world's foremost poets, scholars, and educators. The house, with furnishings from Longfellow's time, is administered by the U.S. National Park Service and is open seasonally. ❱ **Turn left onto Brattle Street.**

Brattle Street (6) has a wealth of single-family houses, richly varied in scale and detail. The *Thomas Lee House (7)* at 153 Brattle Street was built in 1803; it's a white, two-story, hip-roof house with a widow's walk, painted brick chimneys, and an ornamental fence. Here, local builders clung to eighteenth-century design traditions even as new designs were appearing in Boston.

Parts of the *Hooper–Lee–Nichols House (8)* at 159 Brattle Street date to 1685—notably the massive 12-foot square chimney. Extensive eighteenth-century remodeling added a third floor. Owner Joseph Lee, and six other nearby families connected with the Lees by marriage, held strong anti-Revolutionary opinions, giving Brattle Street the name of Tory Row. The Cambridge Historical Society invites the public into the building frequently. ❱ **Turn left onto Elmwood Avenue.**

At 33 Elmwood is the Federal-style mansion called *Elmwood (9)*. Built in 1767, it was home to Elbridge Gerry, Constitution signer and namesake of *gerrymandering*—the delineation of voting districts to favor one electoral candidate. A later resident, James Russell Lowell, poet, critic, and editor of the *Atlantic Monthly*, was American minister to Spain and ambassador to England. Elmwood is now the residence of Harvard University's president.

Across the street is the 1767 *Watson House (10)*, framed with posts and beams that allowed walls to be slender and non-weight-bearing, with 4-inch boards flat against the wall—exactly the opposite of today's buildings. Windowsills protrude outside the narrow walls. ❱ **Follow Fresh Pond Parkway, crossing at the Brattle Street signalized intersection.**

The 175 acres of *Mount Auburn Cemetery (11)*, at 580 Mount Auburn Street, enclose a premier arboretum and a museum of nineteenth- and twentieth-century outdoor sculpture. In 1831 Mt. Auburn combined burials with rugged terrain and picturesque landscaping for the first time in this country. Ever since, this cemetery's romantic landscape designs—as well as its Egyptian Revival gate—have been widely imitated. It's open all year. ❱ **Turn right onto Mount Auburn and right again onto Coolidge.**

The *Coolidge Hill neighborhood (12)* is surrounded by cemeteries and major thoroughfares. The hilltop subdivision was designed by Frederick Law Olmsted, with construction overseen by his pupil Charles Eliot, designer of the Boston Metropolitan Park System. The oldest house is a hip-roof design dating from 1801 at 144 Coolidge Hill. Nearby *Shady Hill School (13)* was founded as the Cooperative Open Air School, moving to Coolidge Hill in 1924. ❱ **Return to Mount Auburn and turn right onto Gerry's Landing Road.**

The first settlers landed on the riverbank just beyond the school at *Gerry's Landing (14)*, later owned by Elbridge Gerry. The *Buckingham, Browne & Nichols School (15)* was formed when the private Browne and Nichols School gradually transferred to this site and later merged with Buckingham School. ❱ **Cross Gerry's Landing Road carefully to the left side of the Eliot Bridge over the Charles.**

The *west bank of the Charles River (16)* lies across the busy parkway. The Cambridge Boathouse (a private sailing and rowing club) is on the left. The bridge, named for Charles Eliot, offers views of Boston's skyline and the Harvard Stadium. Across the river Mount Auburn Hospital has a southern exposure with long vistas. ❱ **Turn left at the Anderson Bridge (the next one along the path) and follow JFK Street to return to Harvard Square.**

Prepared by members of WalkBoston.

Part IV

Long Walks, Paths, and Parks

 **walk 21**

Bridges and Esplanades along the Charles

Start: MBTA Green Line Boston University West Station
Getting there: Take the MBTA Green Line Boston College train
Finish: MBTA North Station
Getting back: Take the MBTA Orange, Green, or Commuter Rail Line
Time: 4 hours
Distance: 5 miles
Difficulty: Easy, with some stairways or ramps
Accessibility: Fully wheelchair accessible
Rest rooms: Museum of Science

FOR A GREAT CINEMATIC VIEW of Boston take a ride over the Charles River on the Red Line across the Longfellow Bridge between Kendall Square and Charles Street Stations. The train accelerates as it leaves the station to meet the rising curve of the bridge, and the short spell of darkness in the subway tunnel dissolves on a sunny day in a flash of blue sky and open water.

This walk takes a longer look at the views of the Lower Charles from a succession of vantage points along the bridge. It encompasses what appears to be one of the most visible and

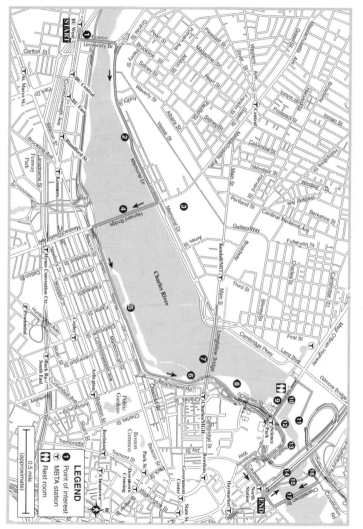

Bridges and Esplandes along the Charles

carefully preserved natural features of Boston. In fact, nothing could be further from the truth. In the mid–nineteenth century the shallow basin was lined with tenements and industries; at low tide it was a vast expanse of noisome, sewage-laden mud flats.

The reclamation of the riverbanks began with the Cambridge Esplanade in 1883 and continues to this day. The completion of the Charles River Dam in 1910 shut out the tides and created the first esplanade in Boston. In 1978 a new dam extended the freshwater basins to the harbor. Work on parks and pedestrian bridges under and around the Central Artery should be completed about 2007, two years after the highway ramps and bridges are finished.

In the meantime, this walk takes in many of the Charles River's loveliest and most historic sites—not to mention its incomparable views of the city.

the walk

▶ **At the MBTA Green Line Boston University West Station, turn toward downtown Boston and follow Commonwealth Avenue to the Boston University Bridge.**

The last wooden bridge on the basin was demolished for the construction of the *Boston University Bridge (1)*, completed in 1928. Underneath it are the two steel spans built by the Boston & Albany Railroad. ▶ **Cross the bridge to the Cambridge side of the river and turn right.**

Charles Davenport's 1870s vision for esplanades along the Charles was first realized with the *Cambridge Esplanade (2)*. In 1883 the present seawall was begun by Davenport's Charles River Embankment Company, and a strip of land 200 feet wide was deeded to the city. Trees were planted and the seawall was completed by the city in 1900, but the land remained largely vacant for the next ten years.

Rejecting an offer to merge with Harvard, the *Massachusetts*

Institute of Technology (3) finally bought some of this undeveloped land along the Cambridge Esplanade in 1912. Four years later a ceremonial barge carried the institute's charter from its old building in the Back Bay to the new campus. ◗ **Cross Massachusetts Avenue and turn right onto the sidewalk on the downstream side of the bridge.**

In 1958 an MIT fraternity measured the *Harvard Bridge (4)* and determined its length to be 364.4 Smoots plus one ear; their unit of measure was a freshman named Oliver Reed Smoot Jr., who was dragged across the bridge. When the bridge was reconstructed in 1990, the "Smoot marks" were duplicated and a commemorative plaque was affixed. ◗ **Just before reaching Storrow Drive on the Boston side, take the pedestrian bridge down to the Esplanade.**

The narrow Boston Embankment, now enlarged and universally known as the *Esplanade (5),* was completed in 1910 as part of the construction of the Charles River Dam. As late as 1928 the *Cambridge Tribune* derided the narrow esplanades and said the Charles looked like "a wash basin with ducks in it." The state developed plans for improving the basin, and Helen Storrow contributed $1 million in honor of her husband, James, leader of the campaign for the dam twenty-five years earlier. Dedicated in 1936, the widened Esplanade was divided by a highway in the 1950s.

The oldest public sailing program in the country, *Community Boating (6)* was initiated in 1936 for youth in Boston's nearby neighborhoods, using plywood boats rigged with bedsheets for sails. The Storrow bequest funded the boathouse in 1941. A junior membership (under seventeen years old) in the program still costs only $1 for the season.

Opened in 1907 as the Cambridge Bridge, *Longfellow Bridge (7)* was renamed to honor the poet Henry Wadsworth Longfellow in 1927. The graceful arched bridge design helped persuade the U.S. Congress to override the federal War Department's stipulation that every bridge below the

Watertown Arsenal include a draw to allow the passage of ships from the harbor.

Charlesbank (8) was designed by Frederick Law Olmsted as the first public park along the river, serving the abutting West End with outdoor gymnasiums for both men and women. Charles Street was widened in the 1930s, and tennis courts replaced the gymnasiums.

After decades of debate and a campaign led by James Storrow, the *Charles River Dam (now Science Park) (9)* was approved in 1903 to stabilize the water level in the basin. The dam was a landscaped park, with a stable and boathouse on the Cambridge side and an open pavilion and gatehouses for the locks on the Boston side. The Museum of Science completed its first building in 1951.

Across the highway from the museum is the 1912 *Green Line Viaduct (10)* between downtown Boston and Cambridge—an early example of the use of reinforced concrete. ❱ **Cross over the highway at the traffic signal in front of the museum's parking garage and walk under the viaduct along Museum Way.**

The granite seawall along the edge of *North Point Park (11)* was built by the Boston & Maine Railroad about 1930 and runs from the viaduct to the railroad bridges. Two new islands create a shallow channel for small boats. A pedestrian bridge is planned to connect North Point Park with Paul Revere Park in Charlestown. ❱ **Retrace your steps under the viaduct, cross the highway, and turn left.**

At the old lock, follow a driveway on the right out to the river and the Washburn Pavilion for a fine view of the Charles. ❱ **Return to the highway, turn right, and take the pedestrian bridge to the Green Line's Science Park Station. Pass through the mezzanine of the station and follow Nashua Street toward Spaulding Hospital.**

Built on land filled to create a parking lot, the central element of *Nashua Street Park (12)* is a granite spiral surrounded

METROPOLITAN DISTRICT COMMISSION

Longfellow Bridge in 1907.

by steam jets. The park offers a good view of the 1930 bascule railroad bridges and the new cable-stayed bridge downstream.

Spaulding Rehabilitation Hospital's riverside pier (13) is used by Spaulding's Adaptive Sports and Recreation Program. Opened to the public in 2002, the pier projects out over the water and is planted with large honey locusts. ◗ **Continue along Nashua Street past the hospital and the Fleet Center/North Station. Turn left onto Causeway Street and walk past the Fleet Center. Just beyond the highway and the cable-stayed bridge is Beverly Street. Turn left.**

The tall cable-stayed *Leonard P. Zakim Bunker Hill Bridge (14)* is asymmetrical in elevation, section, and plan: higher on the north side, wider on the downstream side (to accommodate two cantilevered lanes outside of the cables), and with its back span on the south side shorter than the north back span.

The old Charles River Dam under the Museum of Science was unable to prevent extensive flooding in the hurricanes of

1954 and 1955. The *New Charles River Dam and Pumping Station (15)* were completed just before the Blizzard of 1978, with its record high tides. With a total capacity of 3 million gallons per minute, six 2,700-horsepower diesel pumps pushed the floodwaters of the Charles into the harbor despite the tides. ❒ **Follow the walkway across the locks of the dam past the *Charlestown Bells* by Paul Matisse.** *Paul Revere Park (16)* opened in 1978 as a simple grass oval lined with linden trees. Redesigned in 1999, it features tile panels in its stone walls along serpentine walkways. In the low wall at the back of the grass stage is the text of "The Gift Outright" by Robert Frost. Facing the stone overlook is a ceramic re-creation of a 1775 map of Paul Revere's ride.

In 1786 the first *Charlestown Bridge (17)* connected Boston with the mainland via the North End and Charlestown. At the time it was the longest bridge in America. It was replaced by the current swing bridge in 1899. Though the center span of the bridge is now fixed in place, the turntable and gears of the mechanism are still visible.

❒ **Cross the Charlestown Bridge to Causeway Street and turn right for North Station.**

KARL HAGLUND *is an urban planner and the author of* Inventing the Charles River.

 **walk 22**

The Neponset River and Ashmont Hill

Start: Across the street from the Central Avenue trolley stop

Getting there: From the MBTA Red Line Ashmont Station, take the Mattapan Trolley Extension to the Central Avenue trolley stop in Milton

Finish: Ashmont MBTA Red Line Station; Fields Corner MBTA Red Line Station; or Butler Station on the Mattapan Trolley Extension

Getting back: From Ashmont Hill, take the MBTA Red Line at Ashmont Station; from Port Norfolk, take the No. 20 Neponset Adams bus to Fields Corner Station; if you'll be retracing your steps, take the Mattapan Trolley Extension from Butler Station

Time: 1–3 hours

Distance: 2 miles one-way to Port Norfolk; 4 miles one-way to Ashmont Hill

Difficulty: Easy, with a moderate climb up Ashmont Hill

Accessibility: Fully wheelchair accessible, except for trolley tracks

Rest rooms: Pope John Paul II Park

A QUIET RIVER flows through a widening estuary to Boston Harbor, past riverfront communities and a public beach. This river—the Neponset—is a little-known sister of the larger Charles River. The two rivers could not be more different. Where the Charles is the focus of downtown and the universities, the Neponset flows past old chocolate mills and historic residential areas through one of the last remaining salt marshes and wildlife sanctuaries at the edge of Boston Harbor.

Along the river the Lower Neponset River Trail, a new 2.5-mile pathway built by the Metropolitan District Commission, follows the route of the former Dorchester & Milton Branch Railroad. This trail is reachable by quaint and colorful 1950s-era trolleys that take passengers from the MBTA Ashmont Red Line Station to the beginning of the path at Central Avenue in Milton. From here, the paved footway follows the river past warehouses, mill falls, and a gradually expanding tidal estuary with tall saltwater-washed grasses.

The estuary served as a shipbuilding center as early as 1640. Now, in the face of ever increasing urbanization, it is critical both as a nursery of wildlife and as a respite for city dwellers. Environmental improvements at a 65-acre park, opened in 2001 on the site of a former drive-in theater and city dump, include a magnificently restored salt marsh.

From this marsh you have many options for concluding your walk, depending on how far you'd like to go and what you'd like to see. You might wish to retrace your steps—or take public transportation back to your starting point—for a peaceful riverside stroll. If you opt to continue, the walk leads into the quirky residential enclave of Port Norfolk, along Tenean Beach, and through the historic Ashmont Hill neighborhood for a sampler of Boston both wild and domestic.

A few caveats are in order before you embark on this walk. There are no signals at Granite Avenue; crossing is hazardous for pedestrians. Water is available only at one water fountain at Pope John Paul II Park. Parts of the path are secluded—and the trail closes at dusk—so take a friend along and enjoy your

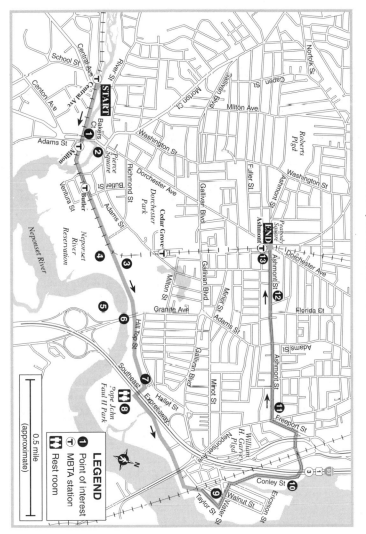

The Neponset River and Ashmont Hill

LEGEND

1 Point of interest
Ⓣ MBTA station
[✚] Rest room

0.5 mile
(approximate)

walk in the daylight hours. Before you begin you may want to review the options for a return walk to help plan your visit.

🚶 the walk

▶ **The path begins across the street from the MBTA station. Head east.**

The river's *geological setting (1)* is visible along the walk. A large outcropping of Cambridge slate lies in front of some picturesque old mill buildings and a tall chimney. On the opposite bank of the river near a redecked railroad bridge are outcrops of Roxbury conglomerate bedrock. The sounds of falling water can be heard through shrubs and trees.

Around the next MBTA trolley station (Milton) are the old *Baker's Chocolate Mills (2),* which once included seven mills on 14 acres. The mill complex, now converted to residential purposes, can be seen by climbing the stairs at the trolley station. Here the river was dammed as early as 1635, when Israel Stoughton built a water-powered mill at a fordable riverside location. Early in colonial history it became the place where the old coast road between Boston and Plymouth crossed the river. The chocolate mills center on Pierce Square, a lively commercial area with restaurants and other retail outlets.

Cedar Grove Cemetery (3), named for the cedar trees that thrived in the fields along the river, opened in 1868. The cemetery abuts the path and the MBTA line, which cuts through it. The Butler Avenue Trolley Station has an information kiosk and overview of the entire Lower Mills district.

Passing under the MBTA trolley, you will see the *Neponset River Salt Marsh (4),* a beautiful wetland surrounding the estuary. The vista opens to spectacular wetlands, said to be the largest intact salt marsh within Boston proper. The marsh is part of the Neponset River Reservation, an integral element of the MDC's regional park system.

On the opposite side of the river, the *Granite Railroad (5)—*

the country's first commercial railroad—traveled from Quincy's quarries to piers on the Neponset's banks, where enormous, heavy granite blocks could be transported by water to construction sites around the area. The railroad was constructed in 1826 as a safe and cost-effective experiment in moving the granite to market. Rails on supporting "sleepers," also of granite, provided an efficient way to transport stones. The carts laden with stone were first pulled by teams of horses and later by steam locomotives when it became a branch of the Old Colony Railroad. The right of way is now mostly covered by the Southeast Expressway (I-93), but the pier remains at the river's edge.

The *Granite Avenue Drawbridge (6)*, first built in 1837, is the next landmark. If you are lucky, the drawbridge may go up while you are nearby. There is an informational kiosk here, as well as benches and a small public parking area. ❱ **Take care in crossing this street, as there is no signal. For safety, you might want to divert from the path and go left for one block to the signalized crossing at Hilltop Street.**

The former factory used by the Keystone Camera Company and a piano manufacturing company has been transformed for residential use; it is now the *Keystone Apartments (7).* ❱ **Turn right and pass under the expressway and turn left; from here resume your northeastward walk.**

Pope John Paul II Park (8) has captivating views of the river as it widens dramatically toward the harbor. At this new $10 million, 66-acre park, paths branch off and loop close to the riverbank and newly restored salt marshes. The park site, once a drive-in theater and a city landfill, has become popular for its ball fields, benches that welcome walkers, and pagoda-like sheds for picnics.

Once mostly tidal flats, the *Port Norfolk neighborhood (9)* was gradually filled in to form an upland peninsula. Today it is surrounded by water on three sides, where the Neponset River Estuary meets Boston Harbor.

The Neponset River Estuary.

▶ If you wish to end your walk at this point, retrace the path to the Butler Trolley Station, or take a bus from Neponset Circle to the MBTA Fields Corner Station. (Note that bus service from Neponset Circle is infrequent on weekends.)

▶ To continue on the Ashmont Hill part of the walk, turn right, follow Taylor Street north, then turn left onto Water Street. After about two blocks, Water Street turns slightly right and becomes Conley Road.

Conley Road leads into the park at *Tenean Beach (10)*, which borders a harbor cove. The sandy beach, recently enlarged with 4,400 tons of sand, offers outstanding views of downtown Boston and the harbor. ▶ **Follow Conley Road to Morrissey Boulevard, which can be crossed at the Freeport Street signals or via the pedestrian overpass near Stop & Shop on the right.**

Follow Freeport Street to *St. Ann's Catholic Church and School (11),* founded in 1889. Ashmont Street, the westward continuation of Freeport Street, climbs the gentle slope of Ashmont Hill, with its variety of homes, churches, and architectural styles of the nineteenth and twentieth centuries. Three-deckers predominate on the ascent. At the intersection of Adams Street is the modified Tudor First Baptist Church with prominent stained-glass windows.

Ashmont Hill (12) was farmland until the mid-1800s, and now includes 40 acres of late-nineteenth-century homes. After Boston annexed the area, the first large subdivision—Welles Hill—was laid out in 1872. Growth was sparked by streetcar lines. On the right at Louis Terrace is a striking modified Greek Revival home with double chimneys. As you near the top of the hill, you will see more Greek Revival and Victorian homes scattered along Ashmont Street and the side streets.

All Saints Church (13) at 209 Ashmont Street was the first church designed by Boston architect Ralph Adams Cram (1892). All Saints is also valued for the extensive collection of ecclesiastical art within its unique carved-oak and hewn-stone interior.

▶ **At Dorchester Avenue, turn left. The MBTA's Ashmont Station is straight ahead.**

MARIA JANE LOIZOU *is a librarian, professional singer, and avid walker.*

 **walk 23**

South Bay
Harbor Trail

Start: MBTA Ruggles Orange Line Station
Getting there: Take the MBTA Orange Line to Ruggles
Station
Finish: MBTA South Station
Getting back: Take the MBTA Commuter Rail Line or sub-
way from South Station
Time: 3 hours
Distance: 4 miles
Difficulty: Mostly flat, walkable surfaces
Accessibility: Fully wheelchair accessible
Rest rooms: South Station

THE SOUTH BAY HARBOR TRAIL is very much a work in
progress—as well as an ambitious and exuberant entry into
the list of Boston's paths. Leading from inner-city neighborhoods to the harbor, some segments of the path are completed, while other parts are being built, and still others
depend on construction help from abutting parcels. The path
was initially made possible by focusing on links with large-
scale transportation facilities. One section of it was created
during construction of the Orange Line through the South
End and Roxbury; another part parallels the Big Dig/Central
Artery construction that affects so much of central Boston.

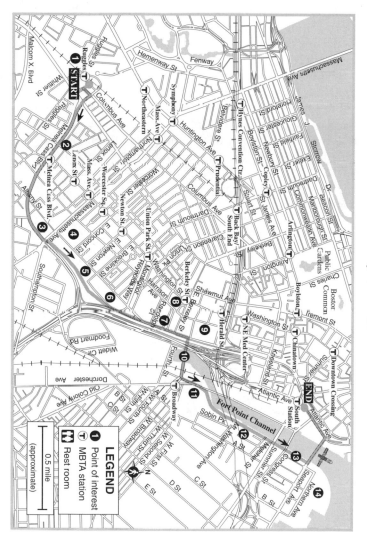

South Bay Harbor Trail

LEGEDN

- ❶ Point of interest
- Ⓣ MBTA station
- 🚻 Rest room

0.5 mile
(approximate)

Yet another part relates to reconstruction of the South Boston waterfront. Along the route of this walk you will see the effects of this construction, as parts of the path are linked to complete a continuous walking route through Roxbury and the South End to Boston Harbor.

The South Bay Harbor Trail is being developed by the South Bay Harbor Trail Coalition in partnership with the city of Boston and the environmental advocacy group Save the Harbor Save the Bay. The plan for the completed Harbor Trail is to connect many of Boston's inland neighborhoods to the expanding amenities of Boston Harbor such as the New England Aquarium, the Children's Museum, and the new Harbor Islands National Park. This major connection is planned to be an attractive route for walking, while functioning as access through a relatively unexplored area on the fringes of downtown Boston.

The South Bay Harbor Trail is also closely linked to walks along Boston Harbor and the Charles River in this book. By connecting this walk to the downtown Harborwalk and Charles River stroll, you can completely encircle the outer edges of downtown Boston, including the South End, Chinatown, the shopping and financial districts, Government Center, the North End, Beacon Hill, and the Back Bay.

The 3.4-mile trail begins at the MBTA's Ruggles Orange Line Station in Boston's Roxbury neighborhood and follows the edge of the South End and Fort Point Channel communities until it reaches the harbor waterfront in South Boston. By carving out a path through a relatively unexplored area, it represents a new approach to urban walks.

🚶 the walk

Ruggles Station (1) is part of the relocation of the Orange Line from Washington Street into a trench route decked for recreation uses. The nearby area is populated with students from Northeastern University and the Wentworth Institute of Technology. ▶ **Leave Ruggles Station and turn left on the Southwest Corridor Path to Columbus Avenue.**

Across Columbus Avenue is the beginning of *Melnea Cass Boulevard (2)*. The left side has pedestrian and bicycle trails leading toward the ocean. The boulevard was named for a Roxbury community activist who successfully fought expressway construction proposed to blanket the area.

At Harrison Avenue the trail becomes a sidewalk. After crossing Hampden Street, it runs adjacent to the new *Crosstown Center (3)* development parcel. When completed, the Crosstown development will include both a walkway and bikeway with appropriate landscaping. ▶ **Carefully cross busy Massachusetts Avenue**.

The Harbor Trail proceeds straight along the right side of the I-93 Connector, part of the Big Dig/Central Artery reconstruction. Notice the adjacent *Boston Medical Center (4)*, a combination of Boston City Hospital and BU's University Hospital. At the edge of the expanding *BioSquare medical research campus (5)*, extensive landscaping and new tree plantings will follow along this sidewalk.

Near the *Boston Flower Exchange (6)*, the sidewalk narrows to a less green and less comfortable alignment adjacent to I-93. Tall fencing and Jersey barriers give this stretch a formidable feel. To avoid future conflicts between pedestrians and cyclists, walkers will be diverted just prior to this stretch of trail to ample sidewalks along nearby Albany Street. Here new landscaping will complement the completed trail scheme. ▶ **In the South End, cross Albany Street at signalized crosswalks. Upon crossing, turn right.**

Boston's *Rotch Park (7)* is a major gateway for future Harbor Trail users. The surrounding *Old Dover Street neighborhood (8)* is increasingly popular among artists and designers. Although the new elevated artery is complete in this area, a temporary elevated roadway remains and obscures much

BOB BERGMAN, MARKETING IMAGES

Boston's Fort Point Channel.

daylight along this portion of the trail. ❯ **Proceed north along the west side of Albany Street.**

The *Pine Street Inn (9),* on the left, is a homeless shelter identifiable by its Italian campanile. ❯ **Cross East Berkeley Street and proceed to Traveler Street, which links directly to Broadway Bridge. Turn right to cross Albany Street and then Frontage Road to reach the Broadway Bridge.**

The new *Broadway Bridge (10)* spans the head of the Fort Point Channel. Built as part of the Central Artery Project, it replaced a mid-nineteenth-century bridge. Well illuminated and wheelchair accessible, it offers interesting views of downtown Boston and the South Station Rail Yards. ❯ **At the South Boston end of the Broadway Bridge, turn sharp right to Foundry Street, where you can pass under Broadway. Follow Foundry Street, cross Dorchester Avenue, and turn left.** At the *Gillette Company manufacturing plant (11),* trees line a vast parking area that fronts the Fort Point Channel.

The *Fort Point Channel waterfront (12),* to be completed

by autumn 2003, includes an 18-foot-wide Harborwalk ease-ment for pedestrians and bicyclists. This landscaped Harbor-walk will link to existing walks along the Fort Point Channel and Boston Harbor. The Harbor Trail will overlap the Harborwalk system to reach key attractions such as the *Children's Museum (13)* and *John Moakley Federal Courthouse (14)* on the South Boston Waterfront.

▶ **Turn left at Northern Avenue and cross the Fort Point Channel. Turn left onto Atlantic Avenue.**

The walk ends at South Station.

MICHAEL TYRRELL *founded the idea of the South Bay Harbor Trail Coalition and is working diligently to get the trail into place.*

 **walk 24**

Southwest Corridor Park

Start: MBTA Forest Hills Station
Getting there: Take the MBTA Orange Line
Finish: Back Bay MBTA/Amtrak Station
Getting back: Take the MBTA Orange Line at Back Bay
   Station
Time: 3 hours
Distance: 4.5 miles
Difficulty: Easy
Accessibility: Fully wheelchair accessible
Rest rooms: Back Bay MBTA/Amtrak Station

THE SOUTHWEST CORRIDOR PARK was almost a highway. On this walk you can see what happened when the expressway plan was dropped, the narrow corridor became transit lines, and a park was built around it.

The never-built Southwest Expressway would have continued I-95 from Route 128 to downtown Boston, replacing the commuter and Amtrak rail line embankment. Hundreds of businesses and homes between Forest Hills and the South End were demolished in the 1960s to prepare for the new highway. As demolition progressed, however, community residents and activists lobbied in protest. Governor Francis Sargent reexamined the issue and announced his decision in

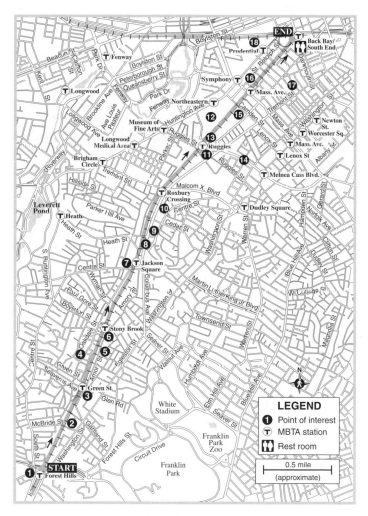

Southwest Corridor Park

1972: no road. Funding set aside for I-95 was transferred to public transportation, the first such transfer in the country. The Orange Line—then an elevated line on Washington Street—was relocated into the underground rail corridor.

The state and the community jointly planned for this huge swath of vacant land. Ultimately it was decided to depress the rail lines; a 52-acre linear surface park was added on top, with walking and biking trails, playing fields, recreation facilities, new housing, and institutions such as Roxbury Community College. Facilities along the corridor were all planned in accordance with neighborhood needs and desires. An overall design gave a uniform character to the landscape.

Completed in the late 1980s, the Southwest Corridor Park boasts separate pathways for walkers and bicyclists. Because the walking path is generally narrower than the bike path— sometimes just a sidewalk—the bike path is typically popular for walking as well but should be used with caution. Walkers should watch for bikers on the bike path.

Large granite blocks from the old embankment edge planters along the way, while kiosks offer maps and historic information. Urban Arts, a nonprofit company, developed artwork specific for every station and created the Literature Project—granite sculptures with neighborhood-based poetry, messages, and letters.

Perhaps best of all, however, is the access that the Southwest Corridor Park affords to the rapid-transit line beneath it. You can begin at, say, Forest Hills, and then follow the corridor to complete your stroll at any station you like. Usually completion of the walk comes at just the right moment—when walkers are beginning to feel tired, thirsty, or hungry!

the walk

▶ **From the MBTA Forest Hills Station, cross under the street viaduct to the beginning of the path.**

Leaving Forest Hills, you shortly spot views of the John Hancock and Prudential Towers. Be sure to turn around to admire the clock tower of the *MBTA Forest Hills Station (1)*. This is a major transportation node, with connections to the nearby Arnold Arboretum, Franklin Park, and Forest Hills Cemetery—all gems among Boston's parks and open spaces. This first section of parkland offers a wide grassy field and is dotted with small community gardens.

At McBride Street, *Boston English High School (2)* is an industrial building rehabbed for education. This location, like more than a mile of the corridor, has been decked over the rail lines for much-needed recreation space. As you cross Williams Street, look to the right across the ball fields to Washington Street, where the elevated Orange Line ran for close to a hundred years. Doyle's Café, at the corner of Washington and Williams Streets, is one of Jamaica Plain's and Boston's famous watering holes, frequented by locals, tourists, and politicians.

The path on the next block to the *MBTA Green Station (3)* is narrow yet still nicely landscaped. After crossing Green Street, look left for Johnson Playground with basketball courts, tot lots, a baseball field, and a wading pool. The path continues up the right side of the tracks, but you may want to walk up *Oakdale Street (4)*, whose elevation offers a nice view of the neighborhood. Look across the tracks for artists' lofts on former foundry and scrap yards. At *Minton Street (5)* are community gardens and a tot lot where Jamaica Plain's annual Spring Wake Up the Earth Festival has taken place for more than twenty years.

Stony Brook Station (6) is named for a hidden underground stream running through the corridor. *Centre Street (7)* is a main commercial thoroughfare and one of Boston's many famous wandering streets. Jackson Square, a bus hub and Orange Line stop, was a lively commercial hub until it was cleared for the planned I-95. *Columbus Avenue (8)*, a six-lane thoroughfare that to some degree replaced I-95, joins the corridor at Jackson Square. Basketball courts sometimes seem to have games going almost 24/7. Heath Street once hosted quite a few German breweries, many of which can still be seen.

Continuing north, you'll see the *Dudley Mansion (Nathaniel Askia House) (9)*, built as an early suburban estate in the 1820s and now run as a private halfway house. Just beyond, look for the 1869 Roxbury Standpipe on Fort Hill.

Ahead and across Columbus Avenue is *Roxbury Community College (10)*, a result of community and city sponsorship during the Southwest Corridor planning. At the MBTA Roxbury Crossing Station a large sign describes the recent history of the corridor and lists local people instrumental in that transformation. From here you also see the modern Reggie Lewis Track and Athletic Center, another of the developments built on state-owned land left over from the highway takings. Halfway through this stretch is Cedar Street, which leads to the Boston Building Materials Cooperative, a resource for tenants, homeowners, and tradespeople.

After you cross Tremont Street, the park widens slightly. The path goes behind the new *Boston Police Headquarters (11)*. Rail tracks are decked over here to provide basketball courts and other recreational space. The recently rebuilt Mission Hill housing is to the west. Beyond the police headquarters is Ruggles Street, a major crosstown thoroughfare. Be sure to use the pedestrian signal here: sightlines are poor, and traffic is heavy. Just to your left is Wentworth Institute of Technology, and a short walk beyond lie Huntington Avenue, the Museum of Fine Arts, and the Longwood Medical/Academic Area.

The campus of *Northeastern University (12)* begins here. Founded by the YMCA, it is now the largest private college in the country. The grand *MBTA Ruggles Station (13)*, a major bus and rail terminal, links Lower Roxbury and the Fenway

Southwest Corridor Park.

through Northeastern's campus. The removal of the railroad embankment led Northeastern to expand its campus and dormitories across the tracks into Lower Roxbury.

Ruggles Station stands at the end of *Melnea Cass Boulevard (14)*, a remnant of an eight-lane Inner Belt highway cutting through Roxbury, the Fenway, Brookline, Cambridge, Somerville, and Charlestown to link I-93 and the Southeast Expressway. A 60-acre interchange was planned for this area.

Beyond the Northeastern University parking lots and garages, the path continues along the Columbus Avenue sidewalk past the ball fields at the *William E. Carter Playground (15)*, which are very busy on summer afternoons. ▌ **From here the Southwest Corridor path is not marked. Turn left at Camden Street after the tennis courts, then right through a small parking lot winding up to the MBTA Massachusetts Avenue Station.** *Warning*: Be careful crossing Massachusetts Avenue at this busy unsignalized midblock street crossing.

The Southwest Corridor Park borders the *St. Botolph Street Neighborhood (16)* on the left, built by speculators in the late 1800s and featuring a variety of interesting architecture. The *South End (17)* is on the right. Streets from both neighborhoods back up to the park, but most do not cross it. The sidewalk path wanders through here with many plantings cared for by neighborhood residents. Where West Newton Street crosses the park, you'll find the lovely Titus Sparrow Park behind the Union United Methodist Church.

At West Newton Street, the *Prudential Center (18)* is one block to the left. ▶ **Continue straight for a third of a mile through the park to the terminus at the Copley Place mall and the MBTA Back Bay/South End Station. Cross Dartmouth Street carefully, as there are no pedestrian signals. From here you can catch the Orange Line, MBTA Commuter Rail, or Amtrak, or take a left into Copley Square, where you can hop on the Green Line.**

JEFF FERRIS, *a citizen participant in the Southwest Corridor planning process, owns Ferris Wheels, a Jamaica Plain bicycle shop.* ANNE MCKINNON *is an urban planner at Howard/Stein Hudson Associates. Both are advocates for walking, biking, and transit.*

walk 25

The Upper Charles River Reservation

Start: Watertown Square; two pillars mark the beginning of the path

Getting there: Take the MBTA No. 71 bus from Harvard Square Red Line Station to Watertown Square; or the No. 70 bus from Central Square Red Line Station to Waltham Center

Finish: Commonwealth Avenue in Newton; or select parts of the trail for loop walks, starting and ending in Watertown Square or Waltham Center

Getting back: Take the MBTA No. 71 bus from Watertown Square to Harvard Square; the No. 70 bus from Waltham Center to Central Square, Cambridge; or the Commuter Rail Line from Auburndale or Waltham (infrequent on weekends)

Time: 5 hours for the complete trail

Distance: 6 miles from Watertown Square to Commonwealth Avenue

Difficulty: Easy

Accessibility: Not fully wheelchair accessible

Rest rooms: Newton's Allison Park near Watertown Square; Charles River Museum of Industry, Waltham

Information: Metropolitan District Commission (MDC), (617) 727-9693; Charles River Watershed Association, (617) 965-5975

The Upper Charles River Reservation

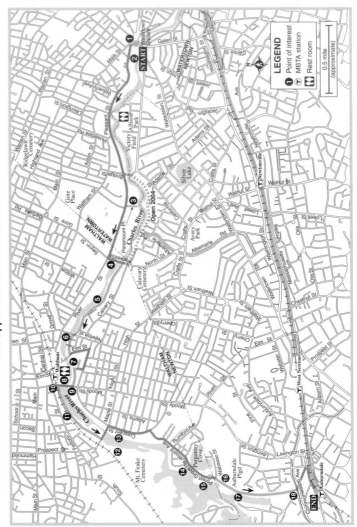

A NATURAL AND WILD quality pervades the Charles River's banks upriver from the dam at Watertown Square. Unlike the riverbanks along the Charles River Basin—the well-known Boston and Cambridge Esplanades with their elegant, manicured walkways and skyline views—the Upper Charles is a narrow winding body of water bordered by a ribbon of lush vegetation. Small dams and arching bridges regularly punctuate this walk, and views of the water are short and focused, extending only to the next river bend, and frequently provided by wooden overlook decks.

The rustic, overgrown appearance of MDC's Upper Charles Reservation is intentional. The greenway is designed to be a self-sustaining natural environment. Even its narrowest sections evoke a wonderful wilderness-like feeling, making the tensions of city life fade. The pathways traverse important songbird habitat, particularly in the bordering wetlands. At the river's edge, adjacent to shallow marshes, painted turtles can often be seen sunning themselves on logs. Forested floodplain wetland supports all this wildlife diversity: tall maple trees provide perch sites for birds such as cormorants, flycatchers, kingfishers, and hawks, which hunt along the river. The expansive tree canopy also provides roosting areas for many birds, including colonies of black-crowned night herons.

This portion of the Charles wanders through Watertown, Waltham, and Newton. Along the river's wooded edges, visitors can jog, picnic, hike, mountain bike, walk, and amble. In the wilder sections of the river corridor, nature observation and bird-watching are excellent. The solitude of some parts of the reservation encourages quiet observation of the water, birds, and gently moving foliage. In snowy winters, cross-country skiers can wind their way along the trails, as snow is never cleared. Upriver from Waltham Center is the "Lakes District," with broad and placid water, undulating forested shorelines, small islands, and a series of intimate coves.

The entire Upper Charles Reservation greenway project is a work in progress, with construction under way until 2004. It is becoming truly the people's river—with something for everyone to discover throughout the year.

🚶 the walk

▶ **At Watertown Square, enter the path between granite pillars etched with a great blue heron.**

Watertown Dam (1) occupies the site where the first dam, a footbridge, was built in 1641 at the head of the tide in the Charles River estuary. Given recent cleanup of pollution, large striped bass are being caught just below the dam, after traveling 8.5 miles upriver chasing and feeding on herring. The dam now includes fish ladders to encourage the fish migration upstream each spring from late April to June.

The migration of blue-back herring, alewife, rainbow smelt, and American shad is a natural phenomenon not to be missed. The *best viewing spot for the migration (2)* is the overlook deck adjacent to the dam. Great blue herons, black-crowned night herons, gulls, and cormorants congregate here to feed. Gulls and night herons signal that the run is under way. ▶ **Turn left onto Bridge Street.**

From the bridge you can see the *dam at Bemis Mill (3),* the only "rolling stone" dam in North America, operated by a rolling cylinder that was easily adjustable to any height. It is different in design, function, and material from other dams along the Charles. ▶ **For a shorter, 2-mile walk, return to Watertown Square on the other side of the river. To proceed, use Pleasant Street for a temporary detour. After 2004, the path will be located on the riverbank.**

At the *Farwell Street Bridge (4)* you enter the south (left) side of the river between granite pillars. Shortly beyond Farwell Street, a secondary path leads to a silver-maple-forested floodplain adjacent to the Charles, a good spot to see herons.

METROPOLITAN DISTRICT COMMISSION

Charles River Overlook.

Not far from the bridge are a small dam/waterfall, a railroad bridge, and a footbridge. The *Bleachery Dam (5)* was constructed for power supply to the Bleachery Dye Works factory, where cloth manufactured in Waltham was shipped to be dyed. Be sure to go over the new footbridge by the dam just before the railroad bridge to a small park on the opposite bank to see the historic sluice.

At the *Newton Street Bridge (6)*, look for the entrance of Beaver Brook into the Charles River. Three blocks past the bridge, a temporary detour is required during construction of the riverfront pathway cantilevered off the side of an old mill.

Back at the riverbank, a *footbridge (7)* leads across the Charles to the MDC's Landry Park. Adjacent to the bridge at the park is the *Charles River Museum of Industry (8)*, a must-see for anyone with even a slight interest in the rich industrial history of the river. The museum is located in the first mill in Waltham, built in 1814, and the first textile mill in the country containing an entire mechanized system from bale to cotton to bolt of cloth. Mills in other cities were modeled on this factory; using the experience of Waltham, the investors and operators of this company moved on to the famous mills of Lowell.

The textile mill used the power of the *Moody Street Dam (9)*, under Moody Street, with its sluiceway and water inlet. The dam, with the biggest drop of any dam on the Charles, has a fish ladder to allow fish to swim upstream to spawn.

Downtown Waltham (10) stretches on the right into Waltham Square and down Moody Street toward Newton on the left. Here you can check out the movie theater, shop, or have a meal at your choice of an extensive diversity of restaurants. ▶ **Cross the river.**

Riverwalk Park (11) is a two-thirds-of-a-mile section of the pathway along the 190-acre water sheet called the Lakes District of the Charles. Glacial activity shaped the surrounding topography into varied and interesting kettle holes and eskers. The trail system wanders through these landforms, offering opportunities to study the geology of the area. At the Prospect Street Bridge, look for the pile foundations for the once famous "Nutting's-on-the-Charles" dancehall, destroyed by fire in 1916.

Notice the *Mount Feake Cemetery (12)*, adjacent to the path at Prospect Street. While not a part of the walk, the cemetery can be entered by respectful walkers. ▶ **Cross the Prospect Street Bridge. Turn right onto Crescent Street.**

The historic *Waltham Watch Factory (13)* was the first to develop interchangeable precision parts for wrist- and pocket-watches sold throughout the country. During its nearly hundred-year history (1854–1957), the company manufactured a total of 33 million watches. Just beyond the Watch Factory, follow a rustic path in the woods along the river. During construction, continue on Crescent Street to Woerd Avenue.

The *Woerd Avenue Boat Launch (14)* allows launching of both motorboats and canoes into the Lakes District of the Charles River. ▶ **Proceed over a bridge. Woerd Avenue**

becomes Forest Grove Road as it leads across islands.

A series of interconnected parks lead toward the end of the walk. *Forest Grove Park (15)* is an MDC facility, one of the prettiest sections in this part of the reservation. A dirt path from the Forest Grove parking lot leads to a footbridge over the *Flowed Meadows Conservation Area (16)* in Newton. Among the small islands of the Lakes District around here, herons, camouflaged by rushes and sedges, use the shallow marsh and shrub swamp habitats to forage on frogs, fish, and other prey. The path through *Pulsifer's Cove Park (17)*, with picnic facilities and a playground, follows the length of a cove off the Charles River. Pulsifer's Cove is one of the last spots in metropolitan Boston where people can ice skate on a river. Hockey nets are placed on the ice under night lighting. Call (617) 965-5253 for public skating information.

At *Commonwealth Avenue (18)*, a short walk to the right leads to the Charles River Canoe and Kayak Center (617-965-5110). Energetic people may want to go for a paddle. On the right is the Norumbega Park Conservation Area, on the site of an amusement park built by a trolley company to create demand for its trolleys. The famous park landmark was the Totem Pole Ballroom, which burned in 1965. In summer sightseeing boats such as the *White Swan* and *Totem Pole* cruised the Charles River between here and the Moody Street Bridge.

◗ **Follow Woodbine Street to reach the Commuter Rail Line's Auburndale Station or buses to Waltham Center for further connections.**

DANIEL DRISCOLL, *a planner at the Metropolitan District Commission, worked to implement the Upper Charles River walkways.*

Part V

Long Walks on the Oceanfront

Deer Island

Start and finish: Shirley Point, at the entrance to Deer Island

Getting there: Take the MBTA's Blue Line to East Boston's Orient Heights Station, where a wheelchair-accessible Paul Revere bus will transport you to Shirley Point, adjacent to Deer Island

Getting back: Take the wheelchair-accessible Paul Revere bus at Shirley Point for the return trip to East Boston's Orient Heights Station and the MBTA Blue Line

Time: 1½ hours

Distance: 2.6 miles

Difficulty: Easy, with some modest hills

Accessibility: Fully wheelchair accessible

Rest rooms: The main guardhouse

Extra features: Make a date to tour the country's second largest wastewater treatment plant by contacting the Massachusetts Water Resources Authority at (617) 539-4102 or www.mwra.com. Between the end of June and the Labor Day weekend you can take a Boston Harbor Cruises ferry from Long Wharf in downtown Boston, near the MBTA Blue Line's Aquarium Station. Boats leave Long Wharf daily at 9 A.M. and return from Deer Island at 12:15 P.M. Costs are around $10 for a round-trip ticket.

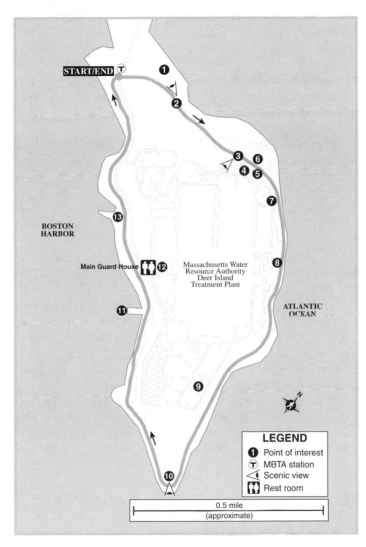

START/END

BOSTON
HARBOR

Main Guard House

Massachusetts Water
Resource Authority
Deer Island
Treatment Plant

ATLANTIC
OCEAN

LEGEND

Point of interest
MBTA station
Scenic view
Rest room

0.5 mile
(approximate)

Deer Island

FROM A HIGH HILL on Deer Island, dramatic views spread out across Boston Harbor. You can see Boston's sparkling skyline, lighthouses near and far, the harbor's twenty-nine other islands, a new windmill at Hull, and open ocean all the way to Europe. At the southern end of Deer Island is a $4 billion technological marvel, a wastewater treatment plant that has ended centuries of sewage discharges into Boston Harbor. The result is water that is cleaner and clearer than any time in the last sixty years.

Despite its name, Deer Island is not an island at all, but a peninsula connected by a narrow road to the town of Winthrop. At one time Shirley Gut, a 325-foot gap, separated the island from the mainland. Wide enough to allow the USS *Constitution* to slip through it during the War of 1812, and navigable as late as 1895, by 1930 the water's high-tide depth was only three feet.

A walk around Deer Island will take you along some of the harbor's most breathtaking and heartbreaking sites. While the views are splendid, Deer Island has a dark side. For 360 years Deer Island was home to Boston's unwanted: quarantined immigrants, criminals, imprisoned Native Americans, orphans, pauper, and the military. The island's hospitals, almshouses, prisons, detention centers, and bunkers were monuments to society's sorrow.

Today few remnants of the past remain, and Deer Island's purposes are to keep pollution out of Boston Harbor and provide a clean, well-tended recreational area for visitors. The island's new 2.6-mile handicapped-accessible perimeter walkway provides one of the best new walks in the Boston area.

🚶 the walk

� The walk begins at the Point Shirley parking lot.

Point Shirley (1), a part of Winthrop, was named in 1753

for colonial governor William Shirley. In the mid-eighteenth century it was a summer resort for Boston's elite. In 1764, when smallpox was devastating the area, Boston doctors opened an inoculation hospital here; in 1776 Royal Marines on the Point fired on continental privateers stealing out of Boston Harbor through Shirley Gut.

By the middle of the nineteenth century, Taft's Hotel (or the Point Shirley House) was a celebrated resort for New England gourmets, with a menu that included hummingbirds prepared in nutshells. It also housed the Atlantic Club, a meeting place for Oliver Wendell Holmes, Ralph Waldo Emerson, Henry Longfellow, and other intellectuals of the day. ❱ **Climb the hill to the left.**

Look back at the *view over Winthrop (2),* a settlement that began when Dr. Samuel Ingalls bought 40 acres of land, laid it out in building lots and avenues, and sold parcels for 1½ to 2 cents a square foot. In 1878 Winthrop's Seashore Home for Sick and Destitute Children began to bring two hundred to three hundred poor children "from the hot and unhealthy streets of Boston and place them in pure air and good influences." Logan International Airport lies directly west.

The *best viewing spot on Deer Island (3)* is the top of the 135-foot hill where you can see the harbor's five distinct geographical areas: from right to left they are the Inner Harbor, Dorchester Bay, Quincy Bay, Hingham Bay, and the Outer Harbor, home to the Brewster Islands and Boston Light. Boston flourished as a port; Boston Harbor was so attractive that, by 1660, virtually all imports from England to New England passed through it to the city's wharves. This hill was originally a glacial drumlin that formed the center of Deer Island. To make room for wastewater treatment plant construction and to shield Winthrop residents from the noise and dust of construction and operations, the drumlin was moved—truckload by truckload—to this northern end of the island. ❱ **Walk down a short distance from the summit of the hill.**

Boston Harbor Islands from Deer Island.

The restored *New Resthaven Cemetery (4)* holds the remains of approximately 850 refugees who died on Deer Island. Nearly two million Irish fled their homeland to escape death by starvation between 1845 and 1850. Deer Island was designated a quarantine station when the numbers of sick and dying refugees overwhelmed the city's capacity to care for them. In 1847 alone, as many as twenty-five thousand traveled by ship to Boston.

Near the cemetery is a small segment of wall, the remains of *Deer Island's military fortifications (5)*. Boston Harbor has always been part of the national defense system. Nets, designed to prevent submarines from entering the harbor, stretched from Deer Island to Hull. Deer Island's Fort Dawes, the harbor's entrance control post, included bunkers with 12-foot-thick walls, concrete roofs nearly 17-feet thick, and a pair of naval guns capable of firing as far north as Gloucester and south to Plymouth. During construction of the new watewater treatment plant, Boston Harbor Project contruction crews used German and Japanese explosives to dismantle the bunkers.

Deer Island's 130-foot-high water tower (6) holds 3 million gallons of water. Below the water tower is the former site of the Suffolk County House of Correction, the last in a series of institutions for the unwanted on Deer Island. The original five-story structure, completed in 1904, was one of the first prisons in the nation built especially for women. It closed in 1991 as one of the oldest continuing penal institutions in the Western Hemisphere.

Upon reaching the bottom of the hill, pause at *two black iron benches (7)*, which face the sea and commemorate two young workers who died in 1999 during the construction of the effluent outfall tunnel. ◗ **Turn right.**

The *seawall (8)* on this side of Deer Island is designed with a concave curve that absorbs some of the force of the waves, controls their direction, and throws them back to the sea. When the tide comes in to the nearby sandbar, called Great Faun, so do charter fishing boats, whose passengers use an irresistible lure made of a long piece of rubber tubing tipped with a hook and a seaworm. ◗ **Continue to walk along the path.** Look at the twelve *egg-shaped sludge digesters (9)* that hold 3 million gallons and stand 150 feet tall. The egg design, rare in the United States, allows digesters to be located on a relatively small piece of land—a fraction of the space needed for conventional tanks.

At the *island's southern tip (10)* you can look across the channel to islands where doubloons and cannonballs lie buried in the sands. A small lighthouse 400 yards out in the harbor marks the dangerous shoals at the northern edge of President Roads, Boston Harbor's main shipping channel. Its light is visible from 14 miles away. Nearby, a stone jetty has invited anglers to the water's edge for decades, and today the fishing has never been better. Farther north, on the left is the *island pier (11)*, completed in 1990. During construction of the water treatment plant, the pier allowed ferries to deliver more than 1.6 million worker trips to the construction site from passenger terminals around the harbor. An adjacent roll-on/roll-off pier brought nearly 222,000 cargo-carrying trucks to Deer Island.

The *old steam-driven pump station (12),* constructed in the 1890s and the only remnant of Deer Island's past, now serves as a visitor center. The station, which operated until 1968, is a Romanesque-style building with Queen Anne details, constructed of brick, granite, and terra-cotta. You can still see one of the original steam engines on the first floor. The 14-by-8-foot-high doors of the old coal-fired boilers also have been preserved and are part of the decor in the building's reception area.

A *memorial to the Native Americans (13)* who died on the island in 1675 during King Philip's War acknowledges their forced internment and underscores the suffering that took place on Deer Island.

▶ **The walk ends at the Point Shirley parking area.**

CRYSTAL GANDRUD *of Dorchester worked on the Boston Harbor Project for twelve years and is now a planner at Howard/Stein-Hudson Associates.*

walk 27

Boston's Harborwalk

Start: Main entrance to South Station
Getting there: Take the MBTA Red Line to South Station
Finish: Commercial Street at Prince Street
Getting back: Take the MBTA Blue Line from Aquarium
    Station
Time: 1 hour
Distance: 2 miles
Difficulty: Easy
Accessibility: Fully wheelchair accessible
Rest rooms: South Station

BOSTONIANS have always had a love-hate relationship with Boston Harbor and the waterfront. We alternately embrace it and shun it; thrive on its wealth and beauty and then pollute and isolate it. But the bond remains.

Over the past thirty years we've started to better appreciate the treasure in our backyard. The wharves are being reborn to lure people back, along with the allure of the aquarium, restaurants, housing, and hotels. The Harbor Islands, forgotten treasures, have been rediscovered. In the past ten years pollution has been cut to a fraction of its former levels. And of course the Central Artery is being replaced with parkland, reknitting the city and the waterfront. To see it all, there's the Harborwalk, hugging the water's edge along much

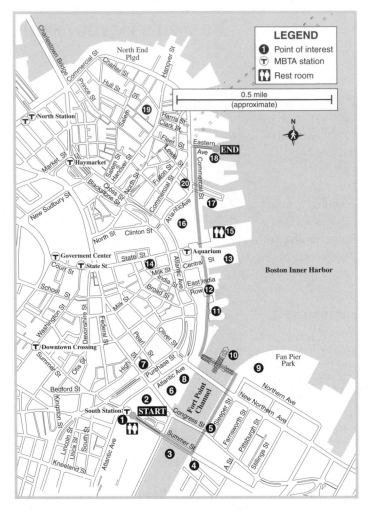

Boston's Harborwalk

of the waterfront, offering views of the harbor up close.

From Boston's earliest Puritan days, the harbor was its life-link with the rest of the world. After all, the city was 200 miles closer to Europe than any other major American port. Its wharves radiated outward like spokes from a wheel, allowing ships to arrive and depart with a vast array of goods from all over the world—West Indies molasses for Boston rum distilleries, ice from nearby freshwater ponds destined for India or Jamaica, and the harbor's famous cod.

With the decline of maritime activities in the twentieth century, the waterfront entered a long period of decline and decay. The Central Artery physically separated it from the heart of the city. The ships and great wharves gradually disappeared. As the harbor slipped from our awareness, we proceeded to desecrate it with pollution and industrial waste.

Now, however, we can again enjoy walking along Boston's waterfront. On this Harborwalk you will experience both the old and the new—not only in the sights you'll see but also in the sounds of the city blended with seabirds' cries and the smell of the ocean.

the walk

▶ **The walk begins at South Station.** When it was built in 1899, *South Station (1)* was considered one of the largest construction projects of its time. In 1916 it was twice as busy as New York's Grand Central Station. Within about twenty years, though, the railroads in America began their long, slow decline and replacement by the automobile. By the 1960s South Station was but a shadow of its former self. It barely missed the wrecking ball.

Look for the nearby *Federal Reserve Building (2)* from 1977, which reminds many folks of a robot with its aluminum skin and tall slender pylons. The missing lower five floors—along with the tower's projecting shades—helps reduce wind downdrafts to lessen impacts to pedestrians. The aluminum skin reflects solar heat. ❱ **Turn right onto Summer Street and cross the bridge.**

Merchant ships once plied the *Fort Point Channel (3)* between the harbor and industries as far south as Boston City Hospital. Today ships no longer use the waterway, and much of the original channel has been filled in. The three bridges spanning the channel were designed to allow ships to pass by. The Summer Street Bridge's center span literally rolled out of the way on steel wheels and tracks (still visible). The Congress Street Bridge is called a bascule bridge and utilized a large counterweight to lift the center span. ❱ **On the far side of the bridge, turn left along the channel.**

The *Summer Street district (4)* is in the process of becoming Boston's "Soho." Many of the former warehouse buildings are occupied by artists. They date to the turn of the twentieth century, when the wool trade flourished, and are still owned by the Boston Wharf Company. Looking down Summer Street, one of the Central Artery's gigantic ventilation buildings is visible, with its wedge-shaped exhaust towers. These structures are designed to keep fresh air flowing in the vast underground highway tunnels.

The world-famous *Children's Museum (5)* resides in a nineteenth-century wool warehouse. The Milk Bottle structure dates back to 1934, when it was a drive-in snack bar. It was moved here in 1978.

Now occupied by nineteenth-century brick buildings, *Russia Wharf (6),* across the channel, was originally the center of Boston's Baltic trade. Russia was an active trading partner starting in the 1700s. The Baltic trade brought us the canvas used for the USS *Constitution*'s sails. William Underwood, father of the American canning industry and Underwood Devilled Ham, established his business here in 1821.

Visible behind Russia Wharf is the *United Shoe Machinery Building (7),* with a gold roof topped with a flag. This 1930

BOB BERGMAN, MARKETING IMAGES

The Milk Bottle Snack Shop, Children's Museum, Boston.

building reflects Boston as the shoe trade headquarters up until the 1950s. Its extreme height, relative to other buildings at the time, reflected a relaxation of zoning laws in 1928 that allowed taller buildings. The previous height restriction was the first such zoning law in the United States; it was challenged in, and upheld by, the Supreme Court.

Along the channel behind Russia Wharf was the *site of Griffins Wharf (8)*, where the Boston Tea Party ship *Beaver* was docked. In 1773 colonists dressed as Indians raided the *Beaver*, throwing chests of valuable tea into the harbor. The ship moored here now is a replica.

The $240 million *Joseph Moakley Federal Courthouse (9)*, named for the popular congressman, was designed by I. M. Pei's firm in 1994. Behind the acre of glass facing the harbor lie twenty-seven courtrooms and forty judges' chambers. From the water's edge you have views of Old North Church, the Tobin Bridge, East Boston, the airport, and Deer Island. During the week don't forget to try out the Courthouse Café—it offers spectacular views of the waterfront! ▶ **Turn left onto the last channel bridge.**

The *Northern Avenue Bridge (10)* is a rare surviving example of a steel-framed operable swing bridge and a symbol of the fast-disappearing maritime and industrial heritage of Boston's historic seaport. The bridge, which dates to 1905, rotated for ships to pass. ▶ **Turn right onto Atlantic Avenue.**

Built in the late 1980s as a luxury hotel/condo/office complex, *Rowe's Wharf (11)* provides unique public access along the shoreline. The arch is designed to allow city views from the water. Its three fingerlike buildings emulate the original wharves found here in the 1800s. Inside the hotel is a fabulous Boston map collection.

Designed by I. M. Pei in 1971, *Harbor Towers (12)* was built on India Wharf; some of the old wharf buildings can be seen across the Central Artery. The first residential redevelopment of the harbor has balconies that resemble zippers. The stainless-steel and buffed-aluminum artworks located at the base of the towers suggest a ship's hull, a dry dock, or a series of sails.

Built in 1970, the *New England Aquarium (13)* was recently expanded to include a 400-seat IMAX theater. The 200,000-gallon circular tank is one of the largest in the world.

The Cape Anne granite–clad *Custom House Tower (14)* was the city's tallest when it was built in 1915, as an exception to then-prevailing height restrictions. It is now a time-share hotel for Marriott and home to peregrine falcons, which feed on pigeons and waterfront rodents.

Begun in 1710, *Long Wharf (15)* remains the oldest continuously operating wharf in the United States. In the 1700s it was the busiest wharf in America and surpassed only by London and Bristol in terms of the amount of cargo it handled. It extends far enough out into the harbor to allow ships to dock in relatively deep water. Before landfilling, the wharf extended up State Street and didn't hit terra firma until several blocks beyond the Custom House Tower. The only surviving pre–Revolutionary War warehouse in Boston is the *Chart House.* The stars on the facade indicate tie rods that hold the walls together. ❱ **Walk out to the end of the wharf.** *Long Wharf Park and Pavilion* function as an emergency ventilation system for the Blue Line subway, which runs directly beneath on its way to East Boston. Toward the horizon, you can see several of the Boston Harbor Islands, accessible via ferries departing Long Wharf. ❱ **Return to Atlantic Avenue and turn right.**

Christopher Columbus Park (16) was constructed in the 1960s and resulted in the realignment of Atlantic Avenue, which originally hugged the water's edge. This was the home base of a bustling fishing fleet before it moved to South Boston in the early 1900s. ❱ **After the park, Atlantic Avenue becomes Commercial Street.**

Granite wharfs were built during Boston's maritime prosperity (1830–60). Most are built of Quincy granite, located on piers to allow direct merchant ship access. Original businesses included sail and rope making, and general suppliers and provisioners for long sea journeys. *Commercial Wharf (17)*, one of the first wharf buildings (1832), was cut in half in 1868 when Atlantic Avenue was built to improve waterfront access. Other granite wharves include *Lewis Wharf* and *Union Wharf*. Between them, the *Pilot House (18)* is an 1863 wharf building of the Eastern Railroad, which at one time provided freight service directly to the waterfront via Atlantic Avenue.

The *North End (19)*, one of the city's oldest neighborhoods, retains some of the scale of eighteenth- and nineteenth-century Boston. Historically the first stopping point for the thousands of immigrants who arrived in the city, it is now becoming gentrified. The first North End waterfront building to be converted to housing was the *Prince Building (20)*, formerly the Prince Spaghetti factory.

⫸ **Retrace your steps on Commercial Street to the MBTA Blue Line Aquarium Station to end your walk.**

ERIK SCHEIER *is a project director with the Massachusetts Bay Transportation Authority and a tour guide for Boston By Foot.*

 **walk 28**

The Hull Peninsula

Start: The Paragon Park Carousel; by boat, debark at Pemberton Pier and begin at number 14 below, following the numbers in descending order

Getting there: From the MBTA Red Line Quincy Center Station, take the No. 220 bus to Hingham, JBL Bus Lines to Hull, or weekday MBTA commuter boats to Pemberton Point

Finish: Pemberton Pier; boaters can end the walk at the carousel

Getting back: On weekday evenings, take the MBTA commuter boat from Pemberton Pier, or take JBL Bus Lines to the No. 220 bus at Hingham to the Red Line at Quincy Center

Time: 4 hours

Distance: 6.5 miles

Difficulty: Mostly level, with one steep stairway and one hill of a moderate grade

Accessibility: Partially wheelchair accessible

Rest rooms: In summer, the MDC bathhouse

ONE OF BOSTON'S best-kept secrets is the pleasure of walking the Hull peninsula—a long stretch of shoreline and flat, sandy public beach that welcomes discovery. The town's relative isolation has contributed to this status: it's out of the way,

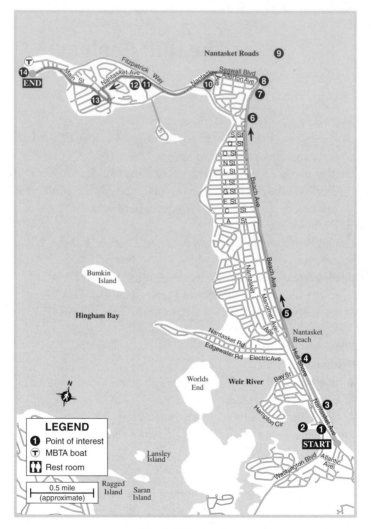

The Hull Peninsula

exposed to the elements, and virtually an island. Another factor might be the town's dual personality. It's called "Nantasket" when the topic of discussion is the old summer resort, with its grand hotels and sweeping verandas, or the contemporary, Styrofoam-cooler-style refuge for day-trippers, surfers, and sun worshipers. (The summer population can swell to more than 30,000 residents and 150,000 daily visitors.) But "Hull" describes the quieter, year-round town and its approximately 11,000 eclectic winter residents.

For more than two centuries Hull was a summer resort, graced with elegant hotels dressed in wide, shady verandas. Expansive summer homes were built on the high, dry hills. Smaller homes sprouted on low, vulnerable stretches between the hills, which to this day are subject to periodic flooding and overwashing when the winds and tides team up.

While the tide changes about every seven hours, beach sand moves along the beach on an annual timetable. Winter storms and currents sweep sand offshore during winter, so on walks between January and May you'll experience a bit of a rockier "road." Spring oceans restore the sand. By summer the beach is back to its smooth, gentle, well-groomed self.

On this walk you'll have a variety of experiences: up-close encounters with the ocean, ample opportunities to exercise your imagination time-traveling to the past, and spectacular vistas. The route passes the entertainments at Nantasket Beach; interesting sea life along the beach dunes; a fort that served the nation from 1776 to 1950; two museums; antique streetscapes; and maritime activities near Pemberton Pier. You can catch a blazing sunrise over the ocean and one-of-a-kind sunsets over the bay. In summer you'll feel the luscious cool ocean breezes; in winter, the rich aroma of salt water and seaweed, sweetened by the cold. Wear your sturdiest windshell if you are braving one of the penetrating winter northwesterly storms, and be careful to stay out of waves' reach in a northeaster.

🚶 the walk

▶ **Arriving by bus, begin at the carousel at Nantasket Pier and Wharf Street.**

The *Paragon Park Carousel (1)*, built by the Philadelphia Toboggan Company, is charming and fully operational (including the calliope), with its original steeds and murals. When the surrounding park was dismantled in 1985, the carousel was saved by private interests.

From 1817 to 1942 large excursion boats brought thousands of day-trippers to *Nantasket Pier (2)* (formerly Steamboat Pier). A strip of summer amusement venues still attracts thousands of Boston-area fun seekers and includes seasonal and year-round restaurants. ▶ **Cross Nantasket Avenue to the boardwalk along the ocean.**

You will be near the southern end of Nantasket Beach. Take in the view. The *MDC Nantasket Beach Reservation (3)*, 1.3 miles of beachfront, has a bandstand for summer concerts and dances, a boardwalk for strolling, jogging, in-line skating, and skateboarding, and a 1930s-era bathhouse with rest rooms, changing rooms, outdoor showers, and water fountains. Bring your bathing suit!

Nantasket Beach (4) is one of the longest (3.2 miles) white sandy beaches in New England. Its graceful crescent is expansive at low tide, and its waves can be awe inspiring at high tide. Members of a local organization, the Drowned Hogs, swim on the first Saturday in February, no matter how cold, raising money for charity and "predicting" that it is still winter.

North of the MDC reservation and its seawalls, the *town-maintained beach (5)* begins. Here dunes, firmly anchored by beach grasses and beach roses and fiercely protected by residents and ecologists, mark the edge of the beach. Behind the dunes you will see the roofs of a long strand of homes built in the town's tradition of extended-family retreats from the city. Each year, more are winterized. From the beach look for

Boston Light.

Boston Light, Graves Light (to the north), and Minot's Light (to the south). As you walk north, Boston Light becomes hidden by a hill but reemerges around Allerton Point.

At the north end of the beach, rocks are exposed at the foot of *Allerton Hill (6)*. Surf-casting anglers prefer this end of the beach for striped bass and bluefish. Cormorants and other ducks are particularly fond of diving here. Irish moss, kelp, and other seaweed tend to collect here, too. ❱ **Find the narrow path leading to the stairs at the beginning of the seawall.**

At *Point Allerton Memorial Park (7),* you may imagine the landing of the 1621 exploring party led by Pilgrim Isaac Allerton. ❱ **Continue on top of the wide, flat-topped seawall.**

From the *Point Allerton Seawall (8)* you and eye-level gulls can take in an island view that includes the Brewsters and the Graves. You are also face-to-face with *Boston Light (9),* on Little Brewster Island at the head of Nantasket Roads, the early channel to Boston Harbor. It was the first lighthouse in America, originally built in 1715. A victim of British reprisals in the Revolutionary War, it was rebuilt in 1793. Graves Light, which marks the entrance to the more northerly channel into Boston, can also be seen. ❱ **Walk along the seawall to the grassy public right of way that leads to Point Allerton Avenue.**

At Point Allerton and Nantasket Avenues is the Tudor-style *Fitzpatrick Home (10),* with a cottage built as a place to play afternoon card games directly on the ocean. Dating to 1900, it was named for its prominent owner "Honey Fitz"— Rose Kennedy's father. It was her childhood summer home.

The *Hull Lifesaving Museum (11)* is housed in the 1889 building where Joshua James began as a volunteer lifesaver and later led Hull's Life Saving Service for more than fifty years. As the station's first keeper, he is said to have personally saved more than one thousand lives.

From the top of Telegraph Hill, *Fort Revere (12)* occupies a strategic location for signaling the arrival of ships. Called Fort Independence in 1776, it was a key communication link during the Revolutionary War; it remained on active duty through the Civil War and both world wars. The Fort Revere Museum is nearby. The old water tower, with its 360-degree vista, is well worth the narrow climb. ❱ **Walk down Nantasket Avenue to Spring Street. Turn left, walk to Main Street and turn right, looping back on Main.**

Hull Village (13), protected from winter storms by two hills, was the town's first settlement. A number of homes and community buildings can be enjoyed from the sidewalk: the *Hull Library,* at the site of the 1644 town parish house, was also the home of Susannah Haswell Rowson, one of the first American woman novelists. The 1889 structure, with original stained-glass windows and hand-carved woodwork, was the summer home of poet James Boyle O'Reilly. The *Joshua James House,* 104 Spring Street, was built in 1680 by an original proprietor of Hull. The oldest house in Hull, *Loring House*, a Cape Cod cottage at 124 Spring Street, was built in 1680. The 1882 *Hull Methodist Church* houses unusual and lovely stained-glass windows. *Town Hall,* built in 1849 as a school and town hall, houses the Hull Historical Society. The *Captain Joseph Cobb House,* 54 Main, was home to a pioneering lifesaver.

The Hotel Pemberton, built in 1880, once stood at the outermost tip of Hull, *Pemberton Point (14).* Arriving guests were regaled with ocean views, breezy verandas, music, delectable food, and an indoor swimming pool. Once known as Windmill Point, for a windmill that pumped water into a nearby saltworks, it has a modern windmill to generate electricity for the town. ❱ **Catch the MBTA commuter boat from Pemberton Pier.**

PAMELA WOLFE *is a community activist in Hull, an outdoor enthusiast, and a transportation planner specializing in public involvement.*

 **walk 29**

Lynn and Swampscott

Start: MBTA Commuter Rail station in downtown Lynn
Getting there: Take the MBTA Commuter Rail Lines from
North Station or MBTA buses from above the Haymarket
Orange or Green Line Station
Finish: MBTA Commuter Rail station in Swampscott
Getting back: Take the MBTA Commuter Rail Lines to
North Station in Boston or a bus to Haymarket Station
Time: 1½ hours
Distance: 2.7 miles
Difficulty: Easy; there are three unsignalized street crossings
Accessibility: Fully wheelchair accessible
Rest rooms: Lynn Heritage State Park Visitor Center;
Swampscott Public Library

NORTH OF BOSTON, the seacoast becomes increasingly rocky and the surf, impressive and invigorating. A favorite walk here traces the expansive and accessible coastline along Lynn and Swampscott. On one side of the 2-mile promenade, the walkway forms a refuge from the tide while giving vistas of sandy beach and waves teasing the rocks and offshore islands. On the other side is a large district of hundred-year-old homes of merchants and industrialists. Residents of this area came here because Lynn was once a powerhouse industrial center.

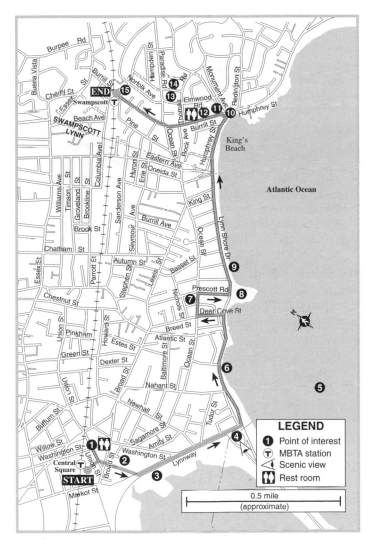

Lynn and Swampscott

Its fortunes began with shoes. Shoemaking began in 1635 as a traditional handcraft, often done at home, but by 1900 Lynn was the shoemaking capital of the world. Nor was footwear the only game in town: Lydia Pinkham's Vegetable Compounds—medicines designed specifically for women— were put on the market in 1876. Heavy advertising brought the firm national renown. Industrial motors and arc lighting arrived soon after with the 1892 formation of General Electric.

Lynn was changed dramatically by the Industrial Revolution and instrumental in the establishment of fair conditions for laborers. Meanwhile the managers of Lynn's great industries lived in considerable comfort in the Lynn and Swampscott oceanfront residential areas.

This walk leads you through the area's industrial history from both sides: you'll see both the remnants of the great, multistoried shoe factories where labor sweated, and the palatial seaside suburbs where management cavorted and unwound. On the way you'll travel past the North Shore Community College, built on the site of other factories, and along the oceanfront—that great leveler and playground of all the people.

🚶 the walk

▶ **From the MBTA Commuter Rail station at Central Square in Lynn, turn left onto Union Street and walk half a block.**

The *Lynn Heritage State Park Visitors' Center (1)*, located at 590 Washington Street, contains numerous historical displays. Exhibits commemorate and publicize Lynn's industrial and cultural history, focusing on shoes, Lydia Pinkham's Vegetable Compound, and the origins of General Electric and the first jet engines. ▶ **Retrace your steps to the station.** Across the street is the *North Shore Community College (2)*, with the

Thomas Magee Building of the College on the corner. On the right is an amusing sculpture dedicated to the industries of Lynn, but looking like a Rube Goldberg design for a dysfunctional railroad. ❱ **Follow trails south through the NSCC campus toward the ocean, to the right of the buildings.**

At the broad street called the Lynnway, yellow footsteps are painted on the sidewalk, leading you to a pedestrian overpass above the busy street and into the 4½-acre *Waterfront Park (3)* that is part of Lynn Heritage State Park. You can walk to the boardwalk at the water's edge for a close-up view of the city marina and the channel around the Nahant peninsula.

The Lynnway leads past boatyards and apartment buildings to Lynn Beach. A large traffic circle marks the beginning of the beach. ❱ **Cross the street carefully to the beach.** Look to the right for a spectacular *view of Nahant (4)* sitting atop the rocks at the end of the beach.

Straight ahead, almost a mile offshore, is *Egg Rock (5)*, a feldspar island rising 86 feet above sea level. The rock was the site of an 1855 lighthouse, burned and replaced in 1906. Like the original structure, Egg Rock Light II helped fishermen navigate safely in and out of Swampscott Harbor until 1922, when it last operated. The lighthouse was sold for $5. When the new owner was trying to transport it off the island, the structure slid into the water and was destroyed. Egg Rock was also the home of Milo, a celebrated dog whose great feats reportedly included rescues of drowning children. Another story told about the rock involves an early lighthouse keeper whose wife died and was frozen. When the keeper was able to reach the mainland in spring, he rowed ashore, held a modest burial, and remarried all in one day, returning to Egg Rock and his lighthouse duties by early evening. ❱ **Turn left.**

In the 1890s an oceanside park was created in Lynn. Transferred to the Metropolitan Park Commission (now the MDC) in 1904, it became the landscaped park surrounding *Lynn Shore Drive (6)*. The road was built for pleasure driving, strolling, and sitting on grassy areas atop its engineered concrete breakwaters.

As you walk along the ocean, notice the two points that protrude from the mainland. The first is Woodbury's Point at the foot of Atlantic Terrace. This broad beach is the setting for a magnificent late-1800s residential area called the *Diamond District (7)*. Homes were built high above the ocean, yet close to the business center and railroads of Lynn. Business leaders built suburban estates in the district and Boston commuters constructed summer residences. Ocean Street is the heart of the Diamond District. ▶ **For a brief visit, turn left onto Deer Cove Street, right onto Ocean Street, right on to Prescott Street, and left again at the ocean.** On the corner of Woolcott Road is a large Christian Science church, a reminder that both Lynn and Swampscott were homes of church founder Mary Baker Eddy.

The largest protuberance of the shoreside park is *Red Rock (8)*, a natural extension of the park out over rocks to the ocean. Now hemmed in by protective breakwaters, Red Rock is said to have been a particular inspiration for Mary Baker Eddy. Sliding Rock nearby was a favorite of children who climbed and slid down in a squatting position, splashing into the ocean. The great crescent of *King's Beach (9)* extends from Lynn into Swampscott. ▶ **Proceed northeast along the seashore.**

As you near Swampscott, you'll notice church steeples and a small commercial area just above the beach. This rocky location is *Swampscott Center (10)*, the commercial and administrative area at the heart of town. A large Civil War monument standing on the shore drive marks the civic center and Linscott Park. The *Town Hall/Administration Building (11)* is located in a seaside mansion, once Professor Elihu Thomson's Georgian Revival home with unique and ornate interior carvings. Thomson founded the Thomson-Houston Electric Company, now part of GE. ▶ **Turn left onto Burrill Street.**

Walking along the seawall, King's Beach, Lynn/Swampscott.

The *Swampscott Public Library (12)* is located just behind the Town Administration Building. ▶ **Follow Burrill Street to the corner of Paradise Avenue and turn right.** The *Mary Baker Eddy Historic House (13)* is located a short distance away at 23 Paradise Road. No. 99 Paradise, the 1637 *John Humphrey House (14)*, is owned by the Swampscott Historical Society. ▶ **Return to Burrill Street and turn right.**

Just to the left of the railroad overpass is *Swampscott Depot (15)*. Built in 1868, the depot is evidence of Swampscott's emergence and growth as a wealthy summer retreat.

▶ **The walk ends here at the depot platform. To return to your point of origin, take the next Commuter Rail Line train or retrace your steps to Paradise Road to take a bus to Boston.**

WILLIAM REYELT *is a resident of Boston and a municipal development specialist involved in housing, transportation, and land-use issues.*

 **walk 30**

South Boston and Dorchester Bay

Start: Columbia/UMass Station on the MBTA Red Line
Getting there: Take the MBTA Red Line to JFK/UMASS Station
Finish: Broadway Station or Andrew Station on the Red Line
Getting back: Take the MBTA Red Line or buses
Time: 5 hours for the full route (Columbia Station to Broadway Station); 4½ hours for a partial route (Columbia Station to Andrew Station); less if a bus is taken on the return route
Distance: 6.5 miles for the full route; 6 miles for a partial route
Difficulty: Generally flat with one significant hill
Accessibility: Fully wheelchair accessible
Rest rooms: Castle Island; two bathhouses on the beach

SOUTH BOSTON has the longest continuously accessible ocean waterfront of any Boston neighborhood; it also has one of the city's highest hills, complete with panoramic views of Boston Harbor and Dorchester Bay. In comparison with the downtown side of South Boston, where port activities dominate, the south side of the peninsula is highly accessible, with many public beaches and walkways. Here active waterfront uses predominate—large public bathhouses and beaches, shaded

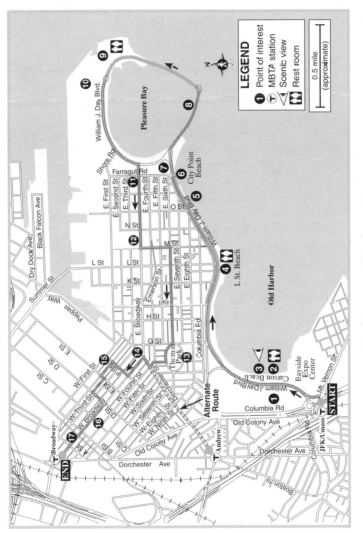

South Boston and Dorchester Bay

pavilions to take in the views, yacht clubs, and fishing spots.

Yet South Boston is as historic as it is appealing. At the end of the beach is Pleasure Bay, a large enclosed basin connected by a pedestrians-only causeway to picturesque Fort Independence on the outermost point of the peninsula. Successive forts have protected the harbor in this location since the earliest years of the Massachusetts Bay Colony. The existing fort is the latest incarnation of fortifications dating back to the 1630s.

Overlooking the ocean on the highest elevation of South Boston is the hill where General George Washington placed cannon to command the harbor and force the British out of Boston. Washington assigned General John Knox's troops to pull cannon from Fort Ticonderoga, New York, to Dorchester Heights during a snowy winter. Once they were in place, the cannon threatened all British defenses of the harbor, and the British left hurriedly on a date since celebrated in Boston as Evacuation Day.

In the 1800s "Southie" began to house immigrants arriving in Boston and gained its well-known reputation as an enclave of Irish Americans. It was both the subject of a romantic song—"Southie Is My Home Town"—and a legendary force in local politics.

As a residential area within walking distance of downtown, South Boston has recently begun to attract young professionals to its quiet streets and older homes. The peninsula lies between the emerging developments of the Seaport/Williams Tunnel District and the mix of new uses at Columbia Point to the south—the University of Massachusetts Boston, the John F. Kennedy Library, the Massachusetts State Archives, the Bayside Expo Center, and new housing. The neighborhood is a wonderful place to take a pleasant saltwater walk along beaches, past pavilions, over causeways and hills—and straight into history, in the form of Boston's best fort.

🚶 the walk

▶ **From the station, cross Morrissey Boulevard, pass behind the state police barracks at the traffic rotary, and follow the path northward along the ocean.**

The large recreational fields of *Columbus Park (1)* are on the left. Beyond the park is the first publicly supported housing project in the United States, named for the mother of John McCormack, former Speaker of the U.S. House of Representatives.

On *Carson Beach (2)* is a bathhouse, with a refreshment stand beneath its iron pergola. Beaches in this area are swimmable for much of the year; storm-surge walls, sidewalks, and street furnishings have recently been rebuilt and improved.

The *vista across Dorchester Bay (3)* shows Columbia Point, once a Boston landfill. At the right is a large mixed-income neighborhood with new town houses. Also on Columbia Point are the campus of University of Massachusetts Boston, the state archives building, and, most noticeably, the John F. Kennedy Library. ▶ **Continue on the path as it curves to the right.**

The *L Street Bathhouse (4)*, a major recreation center for South Boston, contains community facilities. In a well-known winter bathing tradition, the L Street Brownies take their annual New Year's plunge here. Farther up the street is the L Street Tavern—a location for the movie *Good Will Hunting*.

Four *yacht clubs (5)* cluster together in large Shingle-style buildings near boat ramps. The modest pink-shingled home of the late congressman Joe Moakley can be seen across Day Boulevard on Columbia Road.

The next stretch of oceanfront, *City Point Beach (6)*, affords views of Thompson Island (the only private island in Boston Harbor, with an Outward Bound program on the grounds of an old prep school) and beyond to the Marina Bay high-rise neighborhood of Quincy.

BOB BERGMAN, MARKETING IMAGES

Head Island Causeway, South Boston.

Admiral Farragut's statue (7) guards the end of Farragut Street and honors the Civil War hero whose ships captured New Orleans and Mobile for the Union.

The nearly circular tidal pool of Pleasure Bay is enclosed by the *Head Island Causeway (8)*, a pedestrians-only walkway. The seawall here is very popular with anglers. Midway is the Sugar Bowl, a circular concrete sunshade and seating area with wonderful harbor views. You can see Spectacle Island, recently enlarged with soil excavated from the Central Artery Project (Big Dig), and now landscaped to become a recreation destination. At one point this island, formerly a dump and rendering plant for Boston, caught fire and burned continuously for nearly twenty years. Behind Spectacle Island is Long Island with Fort Strong, a former tuberculosis hospital, and training sites for Boston's fire and police departments.

At the end of the causeway is Castle Island, now connected to the mainland. A fort has existed here since the seventeenth century. *Fort Independence (9)* has granite walls greatly enlarged for the Civil War defenses of Boston Harbor. It housed a number of Confederate prisoners of war. Legends suggest that the ghost of an imprisoned officer's widow periodically puts in an appearance. The ramparts of the fort and the surrounding walkways provide superb vistas past Boston Light and out to the Atlantic Ocean.

Next to the fort is *Conley Terminal (10),* the major freight and container port for Boston and the region. Its large, blue traveling cranes are prominent above the ships and cargo.

The *City Point neighborhood (11)* of South Boston starts at the brick bandstand in Marine Park. Several substantial Victorian homes can be seen as the streets slope upward. ❱ **Follow East Broadway, the main thoroughfare, to the right. From City Point/First Avenue, buses go to the MBTA's Andrew or Broadway Red Line Stations.**

Independence Park (12) at the top of the hill overlooks the industrial areas of South Boston and the cruise ships at the Black Falcon Marine Terminal. Handsome brick row houses surround the park. ❱ **Take a left onto M Street to get to East Sixth Street; turn right.**

Directly ahead is *Telegraph Hill (13),* where you'll find the Dorchester Heights National Historic Site and South Boston High School, set in an oval block. Cannon placed on this commanding hilltop during the Revolutionary War forced a British retreat—one of the earliest and most important victories for the colonists. The tower, opened in summer by the National Park Service, has stunning views in all directions.

❱ **From the hill, walkers have two alternatives. You can end the walk at the MBTA Red Line Andrew Station by following Columbia Road to Preble Street. At the intersection of Dorchester Avenue is the station. You can also continue through South Boston's business center to the MBTA Red Line Broadway Station. This extension adds about 2 miles to the walk. Take one of the streets (National or Atlantic) that lead downhill toward downtown Boston and turn right onto**

Dorchester Avenue. The *center of South Boston (14)* is the intersection of Dorchester Avenue and Broadway. Broadway is the bustling commercial core of the neighborhood. ❱ **Follow Broadway and turn right on F Street, then left on West Second Street** to see *Saint Vincent's Church (15)* with its Tiffany windows. ❱ **Return to Broadway via D Street and turn right.**

Amrhein's Restaurant (16) on Broadway is a storied political watering hole, now operated by the same family that owns Mul's Diner across the street. Just before Broadway crosses over the railroad tracks, the *Broadway MBTA Station (17)* contains art exhibits commemorating the industrial history of the district.

JON SEWARD *is president of the Community Design Partnership, a design and planning firm, and a resident of the Fort Point arts district of South Boston.*

🚶 resources for walkers

THE WALKS IN THIS BOOK are just a few available in greater Boston. Cities and towns have established routes for self-guided exploration of their neighborhoods. Government agencies, such as the National Park Service and the Metropolitan District Commission, offer paths through historic areas and parks. Although many commercial guidebooks include suggestions for walks—particularly in downtown Boston—they are frequently changed and thus are not referenced here.

The following is a list of walking opportunities.

Metropolitan Area Walking Opportunities

Regional park and reservation paths, including those in this book along the Charles and Neponset Rivers, Lynn Shore Drive, Jamaica Pond, Savin Hill, South Boston, and part of Nantasket Beach, are managed by the Metropolitan District Commission. Call (617) 722-5000 or (617) 727-5114. Paths in other MDC parks and reservations, such as Middlesex Fells and Blue Hills, are outlined and mapped at www.state.ma.us/mdc/rescrv.htm.

Boston is *"America's Walking City,"* according to the Greater Boston Convention and Visitors Bureau, which maintains an extensive Website list of walks and guided tours throughout the metropolitan region. Contact (800) SEE-BOSTON or www.bostonusa.com.

Boston: Named Trails

The Black Heritage Trail can be self-guided or followed with seasonal narrated walks in downtown Boston and Beacon

Hill by the U.S. National Park Service. Contact (617) 742-5415 or www.nps.gov/boaf.

The Boston Irish Heritage Trail is a self-guided 3-mile walk from Back Bay to Charlestown. Contact (617) 696-9880 or www.irishheritagetrail.com.

The Freedom Trail can be self-guided or followed with seasonal narrated walks by the U.S. National Park Service. Contact (617) 242-5642 or www.nps.gov/bost/ftrail.htm.

The Make Way for Ducklings route from the Charles River to the Public Garden is a seasonal family walk guided by the Historic Neighborhoods Foundation. Contact (617) 426-1885 or www.historic-neighborhoods.org.

The Maritime Trail is a self-guided exploration prepared by the Boston History Collaborative. Contact (617) 350-0358 or www.bostonbysea.org.

The Shawmut Peninsula Walk, with a self-guided map available from WalkBoston, traces the original shoreline of the city when it was settled. Contact (617) 451-1570 or www.walkboston.org.

The Emerald Necklace includes 6.3 miles of pedestrian paths through six parks from Back Bay to Franklin Park. *The Commonwealth Avenue Mall* is a Back Bay connection between Boston Common/Public Garden and the Emerald Necklace. Guided tours in segments of the necklace are offered seasonally by Olmsted National Historic Site Walks (617-566-1689 or www.nps.gov/frla), and Boston Park Ranger Nature Walks (617-635-7487 or www.cityofboston.gov/parks/ParkRangers). Additional information is offered by the Emerald Necklace Conservancy. Contact (617) 722-9823 or www.emeraldnecklace.org.

The Emerald Necklace is connected to several other large open spaces: the *Charles River Embankment* is operated by the Metropolitan District Commission at (617) 722-5000, (617) 727-5114, or www.state.ma.us/mdc/reserv.htm; *Forest Hills Cemetery* (617-524-0703 or www.foresthillstrust.org) is open to walkers at its entrance on Forest Hills Avenue not far from the MBTA Orange Line Station; the *Arnold Arboretum* (617-524-1718 or www.arboretum.harvard.edu), a 265-acre botanical garden with a gate on Washington Street across from the MBTA Orange Line Forest Hills Station, has paths leading through thirteen thousand specimens of plants and trees to hilltop views of Boston.

Boston Harbor Islands

Walking tours of the *Deer Island Wastewater Treatment Plant* are conducted by the Massachusetts Water Resources Authority (MWRA). Contact (617) 539-4102 or www.mwra.com.

The *Boston Harbor Islands National Recreation Area* (www.nps.gov/Boha/index.htm) includes thirty-four islands of all sizes, with several accessible by ferry. Contact (617) 727-7676 or www.islandalliance.org. Ferry services are available seasonally from downtown Boston and from Hingham; call (617) 227-4321.

Brookline

The *Frederick Law Olmsted National Historic Site* (617-242-5642 or www.nps.gov/frla/index.htm) is operated by the National Park Service, offering seasonal tours around the site and along the Emerald Necklace.

For *walks in Brookline neighborhoods,* the Brookline Preservation Commission (617-730-2089 or Roger_Reed@ town.Brookline.Ma.US) has brochures on the Beacon Street Historic District, Cottage Farm, Fisher Hill, the Lindens, North Brookline, and Pill Hill.

Brookline's pedestrian network is detailed in *Exploring the Paths of Brookline,* a book by Linda Pehlke.

Cambridge

For *walks in Cambridge,* the City of Cambridge Community Development Department has pocket-sized brochures on self-guided walks for the Central Square area, Alewife/Fresh Pond area, and Massachusetts Avenue between Harvard and Porter Squares. Contact (617) 349-4604 or www.ci.cambridge.ma.us/~CDD/envirotrans). The Cambridge Historical Society (617-547-4252) presents narrated walks along Brattle Street, and theme walks on other subjects, such as modern residential architecture and works by the country's first successful woman architect.

Mount Auburn Cemetery (617-547-7105) is open to pedestrians within specific hours and offers brochures and maps of self-guided walks.

Dedham

Walks to historic sites in Dedham are sponsored by the Dedham Historical Society. Contact (781) 326-1385 or www.dedham historical.org.

Lexington

Local walking information is available at the Lexington Chamber of Commerce visitor center behind Buckman Tavern. Contact (781) 862-2480 or www.Lexingtonchamber.org.

The 5.5-mile *Battle Road Trail* is operated by the U.S. National Park Service (617-242-5642 or www.nps.gov/mima/brt.htm) as part of the Minuteman National Historical Park between Lexington and Concord.

Newton

Walking routes in Newton neighborhoods, including Newton Centre and Newton Upper Falls, were produced in brochure form by the Newton Historical Commission/Jackson Homestead (617-552-7238 or www.ci.newton.ma.us/ Jackson) in conjunction with the Newton Planning and Development Department.

A history of Newton Upper Falls, *Makers of the Mold,* by Kenneth W. Newcomb, may be viewed at www.channel1.com/ users/hemlock.

Wakefield

Walking tours of Wakefield, including historic lakeside homes, are sponsored by the Friends of Lake Quanapowitt. Contact (781) 245-3282 or www.Wakefield.org/folq/).

Boston Walking Service Organizations

Boston Park Department Park Rangers operate year-round guided walks for children and adults. Contact (617) 635-7487, (617) 635-7383, or www.cityofboston.com/parks/ parkrangers/historical.asp.

Big Dig tours of the Central Artery/Tunnel construction project are offered at (617) 951-6400 or www.bigdig.com.

Boston by Foot offers a variety of guided walks through many neighborhoods, including Back Bay, North End, South End, and Beacon Hill, as well as the Freedom Trail and a special children's program called Boston by Little Feet. Contact (617) 367-2345 or www.bostonbyfoot.com.

Boston GreenSpace Alliance has a Get to Know Your City Parks Program that recently included a walk between 100-acre Millennium Park in West Roxbury and 148-acre Brook Farm (site of an 1840s transcendental community). Contact (617) 426-7980 or www.greenspacealliance.org.

Boston Photowalks offers walking tours for photographers. Contact (617) 851-2273 or www.photowalks.com/general_ information.htm.

Discover Boston provides audiocassette players for walking tours. Contact (617) 742-1440 or www.discoverbostontours.com.

Dreams of Freedom offers historic walks guided by costumed actors. Contact (617) 695-9990 or www.dreamsof freedom.org.

MYTOWN (Multicultural Youth Tour of What's Now) has youth-led walks of Boston's South End. Contact (617) 536-8696 or www.mytowninc.com.

Urban Safaris offers walking tours of South End/Bay Village and the North End. Contact (781) 592-3284 or www.dalemyerowassociates.com.

WalkBoston offers up to twelve walking tours of neighborhoods in a variety of cities and towns each year. For information call (617) 451-1570 or visit www.walkboston.org.

# Index

about WalkBoston

WALKBOSTON, a nonprofit membership organization founded in 1990, promotes walking for transportation, health, and recreation through education and advocacy. Our mission is to create and preserve safe walking environments that build vital communities throughout the Boston metropolitan region.

One way WalkBoston educates is by leading a series of walks each spring and fall, many of which are featured in this book. Walking affords the deepest appreciation of the people, culture, architecture, and history of a community. These walks reveal the joys of sights and sounds experienced only at walking pace, as well as what makes for a pleasant—or unpleasant—walking environment. Walks are designed primarily by WalkBoston members.

WalkBoston advocates for pedestrians by playing a prominent role in improving the design and use of streets, sidewalks, and pathways in the greater Boston area. Working with citizen groups, government officials, and private developers, WalkBoston has dramatically improved the walking experience for all to enjoy.

Among WalkBoston's many accomplishments are a pedestrian-friendly design on the greenway planned for above the new underground Central Artery in Boston; new, automatic, and longer WALK signals in Harvard Square, Cambridge; creating the first Safe Routes to School Program in New England; and forming the Massachusetts Trails and Greenways Network, whose goal is to connect trails to town centers, transit, and schools.

Today the Boston region is better for walking because of WalkBoston's efforts.

For more information on becoming a WalkBoston member, call 617-451-1570 or visit www.walkboston.org.

about the Appalachian Mountain Club

Since 1876, the Appalachian Mountain Club and its members have worked to promote the protection, enjoyment, and wise use of the mountains, rivers, and trails of the Northeast. We encourage people to enjoy and appreciate the natural world because we believe that successful conservation depends on this experience.

Join us!

Hiking, paddling, biking, skiing—from backyard nature walks to week-long wilderness explorations, the AMC offers activities for all kinds of outdoor adventurers. Join the AMC and connect with new people, learn new skills, and feel good knowing you're helping to protect the natural world you love. In addition to hundreds of activities offered every month through your local AMC chapter, you can also enjoy discounts on AMC workshops, lodging, and books.

Outdoor Adventures and Workshops

Develop your outdoor skills and knowledge through the AMC programs! From beginner backpacking and family canoeing to guided backcountry trips, you'll find something for any age or interest.

Lodging

AMC's huts, lodges, camps, and campsites—located throughout the Northeast—offer unique outdoor adventures. Perfect for every kind of mountain traveler.

Books and Maps

AMC's hiking, biking, and paddling guides lead you to the most spectacular destinations in the Northeast. We're also your definitive source for how-to guides, trail maps, and adventure tales.

For more information about the Appalachian Mountain Club, call 617-523-0636 or visit us online at www.outdoors.org.

Appalachian Mountain Club
5 Joy Street ◆ Boston, MA 02108
www.outdoors.org

Leave No Trace

 The Appalachian Mountain Club (AMC) is a national educational partner of Leave No Trace, Inc., a nonprofit organization dedicated to promoting and inspiring responsible outdoor recreation through education, research, and partnerships. The Leave No Trace program seeks to develop wildland ethics—ways in which you can act in the outdoors to minimize your impact on the areas you visit and to protect our natural resources for future enjoyment.

By practicing and passing along these seven principles, you can help protect the special places you love:

- Plan ahead and prepare
- Travel and camp on durable surfaces
- Dispose of waste properly
- Leave what you find
- Minimize campfire impacts
- Respect wildlife
- Be considerate of other visitors

If you would like to learn more about how you can help promote these simple principles, consider the Leave No Trace Master Educator Course. This five-day course is designed especially for outdoor professionals and land managers. The AMC has joined the National Outdoor Leadership School (NOLS) as the sole providers of the Leave No Trace Master Educator course through 2004. The AMC offers this course at locations throughout the Northeast.

For more information or to join Leave No Trace, please contact:

Leave No Trace, Inc.
P.O. Box 997 ◆ Boulder, CO 80306
800-332-4100
www.LNT.org